Helping Students Learn:
RESOURCES, TOOLS, AND ACTIVITIES FOR COLLEGE EDUCATORS

Maryellen Weimer

Magna Publications
Madison, Wisconsin

Magna Publications

2718 Dryden Drive

Madison, WI 53704

Magnapubs.com

ISBN: 978-0-912150-60-4

MAGNA PUBLICATIONS

Contents

Introduction to the Collection 5

Students and Studying: What We Know..7
Introduction 8
A Quiz on Study Strategies that Support Student Learning 9
Study Strategies: What Do We Know? 15
Confronting the Myth of Multitasking: A Collection of Tools and Resources 21
Ask 'Em! How Do You Study?..29
Advice on How to Study: Who Should Give It? 33
Review and Reflection..34
Reflection, Action, and Results 35

Instructional Strategies that Develop Study Skills 37
Introduction 38
Regular, Ongoing, In-class Review 39
Quizzes: What They Do and Don't Accomplish 41
Quizzes: Creative Alternatives 43
Low-Stakes Assignments: Challenges and Opportunities 47
Exam Review Sessions 49
Exam Debriefs...51
Test Review Session Activities 53
Getting Students to Talk about Those Disappointing Grades 55
Review and Reflection..57
Reflection, Action, and Results 58

Note Taking That Promotes Learning 61
Introduction 62
Why Students Need to Take Notes for Themselves 63
A Handout for Students on Note-taking..65
Skeleton Outlines and Partial Notes 67
Two Unique Strategies that Improved Note Taking 69
Discussions and Notes 71
Laptop Zones..73
Laptops or Longhand? 75
Review and Reflection..77
Reflection, Action, and Results 78

Reading Skills 81
Introduction...82
Doing the Reading and Developing College-Level Reading Skills................83
Making the Most of Highlighting..87

Actions that Underscore of Importance Assigned Readings 89

Review and Reflection...91

Reflection, Action, and Results.. 92

Study Groups **93**

Introduction.. 94

Study Groups: A Research Analysis... 95

Student-Run Study Groups: A Model 97

Ways to Encourage Students to Study Together.. 99

Study Groups: They Can Improve Grades and Learning...................................... 103

Review and Reflection...105

Reflection, Action, and Results... 106

Studying for Exams **109**

Introduction...110

How Do You Study for an Exam?...111

A Study Game Plan Assignment for Students... 114

A Study-for-an-Exam Assignment 117

Memo to Students.. 119

Study Strategies Students Use for Exam Preparation 121

Student-Generated Test Questions..123

Exam Wrappers...125

Confronting Exam Performance: Learning from how I Studied 129

Review and Reflection.. 131

Reflection, Action, and Results...133

Developing Students' Understandings of Themselves as Learners **135**

Introduction...136

Before and After Learning 137

Learning Logs 139

Learning Log Prompts 140

An Innovative Post-Exam Review Activity 141

Review and Reflection..143

Reflection, Action, and Results...144

Conclusion **145**

Additional Resources from Magna Publications **147**

Introduction to the Collection

"Few teachers effectively prepare students to learn on their own." That's an observation made by Barry Zimmerman whose work on self-regulated learning is classic. The instructional practices of many teachers would seem to confirm the belief that students pick up those learning skills on their own, more or less automatically. Perhaps, maybe to some degree, but why then are so many of our students such dependent learners? They want us to tell them exactly what they need to do. They look to us for answers and seldom have questions. We see any number of them making poor decisions about learning; skipping class, not doing the reading, cramming, cheating. Most of us are not teaching independent, autonomous, self-directed learners.

That's how I got to the question that motivated preparation of this collection of resources. **Is there anything a busy teacher with lots of content to cover can do to help students develop as learners?** And here my answer, a collection of resources—strategies, techniques, approaches, activities, handouts, questionnaires, assignments, and tools of various sorts that develop learning skills as students work to master course content. Some of these resources aspire to grow your knowledge, make you aware of relevant research findings and identify good sources should you have an interest in learning more.

At the end of the day, education is all and only about learning, and our teaching responsibility is to students as learners. That starts with students learning our content, but it doesn't end there. As important as content knowledge is, teaching students those skills that enable deep, lasting, lifelong learning also matters. On some days I wonder if those skills aren't more important than content knowledge. On most days I'm convinced they're more enduring.

Allegiance to content is strong. We know it; most of us are in love with it. We teach with a strong commitment to pass it on—the quality of individual life and life with others in this shared planetary space depends on our breadth and depth of knowledge. But that knowledge is acquired with learning skills—both cognitive, higher order skills such as critical thinking and problem solving, and basic skills including reading, writing, calculating and studying. If those skills are missing or poorly developed, students don't learn as much of our content and they don't learn it as well.

The stakes are high, but I rediscovered as I put together this collection, there are all sorts of ways teachers can develop student learning skills. We already do so, but often more implicitly than explicitly. It makes a big difference when we teach them purposefully, with goals and objectives in mind. Lots of these resources cultivate good learning skills in small ways, using time-efficient approaches. Many of them are evidence-based. I've made it a goal to select resources that are relevant to teaching and learning in a wide range of disciplines, programs, and teaching situations.

For some time now I've aspired to explore how collections of resources could be assembled into something that looks like a book but doesn't read like one. You're holding my first attempt—a collection of all kinds of different material drawn from the various things I've written, highlighted and discovered in my work for Magna Publications. There're articles that summarize research, materials from various Magna programs, handouts that can be distributed to students, surveys, blog posts, and more, yes even some new resources prepared specifically for this collection.

If you're still convinced books need to be read cover to cover, that's fine, it works with this collection. But it's also organized so you can dip in wherever it looks and feels interesting. You don't have to start any particular place, you don't have to read everything in a section, you can start reading something, decide it's not of interest, and move on. The resources are pretty much free standing although I have included cross-references when there's more than one resource relevant to the topic.

I hope you find these resources useful. We've designed this book in an open layout so you can take notes, make plans, and copy quizzes and assignments to use in your own classes. If you'd like to provide some feedback, be welcome to jot me a note: grg@psu.edu I also hope that what you find here makes you think, wonder, and want to further explore your own teaching more. It's not just about developing students as learners; it's also how learning grows and develops teachers.

And finally, some of you have been reading my work for years. Thank you and my continuing thanks to Magna for making my work available in these interesting and useful formats.

Maryellen Weimer, PhD
Long-time editor of *The Teaching Professor*
May 2019

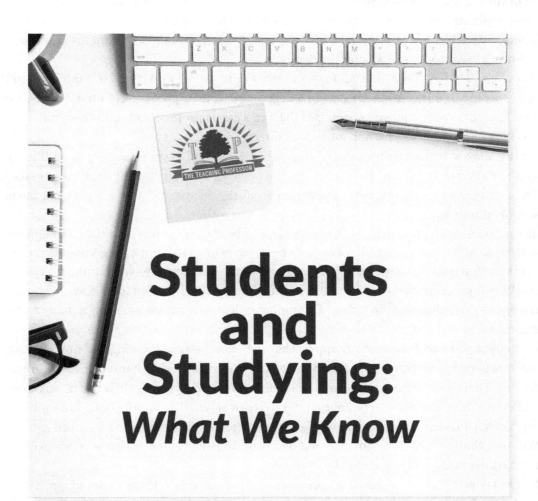

Students and Studying:
What We Know

Introduction

If we're interested in developing students as learners, the most obvious place to start is with their study skills. Many of us teach students who don't have good study skills. It's easy to get sidetracked with who or what's to blame. It ends up there're lots of possible reasons—prior educational experiences or lack of them, little or no self-confidence, lack of motivation, helicopter parents. Some or all may apply to any given student. It's also easy to decide we can't teach study skills; we don't have time, the course is already packed full of essential content, there's a learning center on campus, and when it's said and done, it's a student responsibility anyway.

Studying is how students learn the content, so if they don't or can't do it well, it's our content they end up not learning. If our courses are part of a degree program or preparatory for a degree program, the content students are missing compromises their success as professionals and the reputation of our programs. We almost *have* to care and most of us already do.

None of this makes dealing with students' study skills easy. And despite any responsibilities in this area that we might decide to own, no teacher has the power to make a student study or to make them study in a particular way. Our role is to support their efforts, persuasively, and that's what the materials in this section aim to do.

Our success starts with knowledge—we need to know about the best ways to study and although we do know more than most students, there is some research evidence that may not know as much as we should. This section contains a quiz on study strategies—you can give it to your students. You might consider taking it yourself. The resource collection highlights research that identifies evidence-based study strategies—ones that work in terms of a number of learning outcomes, most notably and consistently, exam scores.

We also know a good deal about study approaches that compromise learning and multitasking is among the most egregious. Our students and the rest of the culture (yes, that includes us) are addicted to our devices. There's evidence in these materials that policies preventing their use in class aren't particularly effective. Students have to figure that out for themselves that multitasking is a problem. The section includes a quiz that students can take and a set research-based answers they can compare with theirs. Will that change their behavior? I'm not overly optimistic but the evidence is compelling and some of our students are still persuaded by evidence.

Finally, or maybe initially depending on your use of these resources, there's a set of questions you can use to find out what your students say about how they study. We make assumptions about how they do. Every now and then we ought to put those assumptions to the test. Questions like these can and let students do the same. Are they studying as much and in the ways others in the course are studying? And last but not least, there's the question of giving students advice about how to study. Do they listen and act on what we tell them? A resource in this section presents an interesting alternative.

This section is the place to begin, to enlarge your knowledge of how students do study and how they should. It provides the background knowledge on which resources in the following sections rest and activities to get you started.

A Quiz on Study Strategies that Support Student Learning

How much do your students know about effective study strategies? Most students think they know what works, but their knowledge is anecdotal, and experience based. Much research has been conducted on study strategies, with some strategies proven more effective than others. Wouldn't students benefit from knowing which ones work best and under what conditions?

There are six scenarios (beginning on page 10) that each describe two approaches. One has documented positive effects on learning. They're formatted here as a quiz with an answer sheet that follows.

Teachers could:

- Post the quiz on the course website and recommend or require students to complete it

- Have students take the quiz and justify the approach they've selected

- Administer the quiz in class and then review the correct answers as a group

- Consider taking the quiz themselves. In research that used these scenarios, instructors did score better than students, but not by much.

These scenarios are slightly edited versions of ones used by Morehead, Rhodes, and DeLozier who gave us permission to share them in this format. The Morehead team scenarios are similar to those developed for research completed by McCabe.

REFERENCES

Morehead, K., Rhodes, M. G., and DeLozier, S. (2016). Instructor and student knowledge of study strategies. *Memory, 24* (2), 257-271.

McCabe, J. (2011). Metacognitive awareness of learning. *Memory and Cognition, 39* (3), 462-476.

GENERATION

Two assignments ask students to learn the list of cranial nerves. Both recommend using a mnemonic device to do so. In one of the assignments the instructor provides a common mnemonic that students are welcome to use. In the other assignment students are to create their own mnemonic device and use it to memorize the nerves. After two weeks, students are asked to list the cranial nerves in order. Which mnemonic device is more likely to help students remember the list of nerves?

1. The one provided by the teacher

2. The ones students created

Briefly explain the rationale behind your choice:

LOW-INTEREST VERSUS HIGH-INTEREST DETAILS

Two multimedia slide shows present information about the same scientific topic. Both contain information directly relevant to the topic. Both also contain other details that are not relevant and that students won't be tested on. In one of the slide shows, the irrelevant details are ones most college students will find highly interesting. In the other slide show the details aren't of great interest to college students. After having a chance to study these materials, students take a test that asks how the scientific topic applies to new situations. Which slide show will help students more when they study and take the test?

1. The slide show with interesting irrelevant details

2. The slide show with uninteresting irrelevant details

Briefly explain the rationale behind your choice:

STATIC VERSUS ANIMATED IMAGES

Two presentations describe information relevant to a scientific topic. The first presents the information in paper form. It includes printed illustrations along with the text. The second presentation is computer-based and includes video illustrations. After an opportunity to study the material, students are asked to provide a written explanation of the scientific principle and to discuss how it applies to new situations. Which presentation method will be more helpful to students?

1. The information presented as printed text with illustrations

2. The information presented as computer-based with video illustrations

Briefly explain the rationale behind your choice:

TESTING VERSUS REREADING

Students in two different classes are studying a 275-word passage. In the first class they study it for seven minutes and then write down, from memory, as much of the material as they can remember. In the second class, students study the passage for seven minutes and then they are asked to study it for a second seven minutes. After a week, students in both classes are asked to recall as much of the passage as they can remember. Which class will likely remember more most a week later?

1. The class that studied and wrote down what they remembered

2. The class that studied for two seven-minute intervals

Briefly explain the rationale behind your choice:

INTERLEAVING VERSUS BLOCKING

Two art history professors are presenting six paintings each by 12 different artists (72 paintings total). The first professor presents all six paintings done by one artist and then moves on to the second artist, showing the six paintings of that artist, and so on until all of the paintings have been shown (strategy 1). The second professor intermingles the paintings, showing different paintings by different artists until all the paintings have been show (strategy 2). Which approach would make learning the artists and the paintings easier?

1. The approach where all the painting by the same artist were grouped together

2. The approach where the paintings of the artists were intermingled

Briefly explain the rationale behind your choice:

SPACING VERSUS MASSING

Two students are studying for an exam. One student begins studying two days before the exam. The other student studies a little bit every day for two weeks before the exam. Both students spend the same amount of time studying. Which approach will likely result in a higher exam score?

1. The approach where the student studied for two days before the exam

2. The approach where the student studied some every day for two weeks before the exam

Briefly explain the rationale behind your choice:

ANSWER SHEET

GENERATING OR BEING GIVEN INFORMATION?

Generating information is more beneficial to learning than being given the information. Students will do better at remembering things like lists if they create their own mnemonics than if they use those provided by the teacher. When students generate information, it makes sense to them, which makes it easier to remember. This why it's much better for students to take notes rather than being given the teacher's notes or slides.

Key reference: DeWinstanley, P. A. and Bjork, E. L. (2004). Processing strategies and the generation effect: Implications for making a better reader. *Memory & Cognition*. *32*, 945-955.

LOW- OR HIGH-INTEREST DETAILS?

Low-interest details are better than those that are highly interesting when both kinds of details are irrelevant. One might expect the interesting details to keep the learner attentive and engaged with the learning task. But these extraneous details aren't relevant and may actually distract students from what needs to be learned. When the details aren't interesting, they can be ignored, and the learner can more easily focus on the task.

Key reference: Mayer, R. E., Griffith, E., Jurkowitz, I. T. N., and Rodman, D. (2008). Increased interestingness of extraneous details in a multimedia science presentation leads to decreased learning. *Journal of Experimental Psychology Applied, 14*, 329-339.

STATIC OR ANIMATED IMAGES?

Static images are more helpful to learning because learners have a limited number of resources for processing information (think brain power). Understanding animated images takes more of those resources because those images contain more details, many of them extraneous. With still images the learner has more processing resources available and can therefore focus more energy on the learning task.

Key reference: Mayer, R. E., Hegarty, M., Mayer, S., and Campbell, J. (2005). When static media promote active learning: Annotated illustrations versus narrated animations in multimedia instruction. *Journal of Experimental Psychology Applied, 11*, 256-265.

TESTING OR REREADING?

Testing is a more effective approach than rereading, restudying, or going over the material. Having to answer a question forces the learner to retrieve the information and every time that information is retrieved, the more solidified it becomes; ergo, the easier it is remember. Also, when students reread notes or the text, the terms and concepts start to look familiar. That leads students to mistake simply recognizing the term from understanding the term.

Key reference: Rodiger, H. L. and Karpicke, J. D. (2006). Test-enhanced learning: Taking memory tests improves long-term retention. *Psychological Science 17*, 249-255.

INTERLEAVING OR BLOCKING?

Interleaving or learning material out of order, mixed, or intermingled works better than learning material as it was presented or with all the same material lumped together. When studying learners should mix up different kinds of problems or review different kinds of materials within one study session. Even though material is presented sequentially in a course, that's not the order in which it usually appears on exams.

Key reference: Roher, D. and Taylor, K. (2007). The shuffling of mathematics problems improves learning. *Instructional Science, 35,* 481-498.

SPACING OR MASSING?

If the amount of study time is held constant (say four hours), spacing (study in 30-minute intervals, twice a day for four days) is more effective than "massing" (what's more commonly called cramming—intense study the night before or the day of the exam). Why? Spacing means more retrieval practice. The same material must be remembered and recalled multiple times.

Key reference: Kornell, N. and Bjork, R. A. (2008). Learning concepts and categories: Is spacing the "enemy of induction"? *Psychological Science, 19,* 585-592.

Note: Many studies support the correct answer in each of these scenarios. The key reference is an important study that illustrates the kind of research being used to support the effectiveness of the approach.

INTERESTED IN COMPARING YOUR SCORE WITH THAT OF STUDENTS AND TEACHERS?

Students and teachers in the Morehead, Rhodes, and DeLozier study that used the scenarios rated (on a 7-point scale) how beneficial they thought each approach was to learning. What's listed below is the mean percentage of students and instructors who provided a higher rating for the evidence-based approach.

	Students	Instructors
Generation	52%	75%
Low-interest details	19%	8%
Static media	20%	14%
Testing	49%	62%
Interleaving	16%	13%
Spacing	69%	74%

Study Strategies: What Do We Know?

We know a lot about study strategies—how they can be used to improve exam performance and promote a deeper understanding of the material. We also know that many students aren't attempting to learn course content with strong study skills. They procrastinate, have short attention spans, if they read, they spend lots of time highlighting without strong rationales for underlining what they do, and they equate memorizing with understanding. If these are the approaches to studying that don't work, what about the ones that do?

The research enterprise has much to offer. It includes concrete evidence that certain ways of studying are more effective than others. Self-testing, regular review, review of several topics during a study session, elaborating and explaining to others are among the strategies that improve performance on exams and promote deeper understanding and better long-term retention. Teachers can play an important role in helping students develop study skills that promote success in college and translate into increasingly necessary lifelong learning skills.

The resources below comprise a small collection of the work that's been done on study strategies. They are representative of the findings. All the articles include extensive reference section that can lead those interested to a wide range of other studies and resources on study strategies and related topics.

Background: Good overviews of the research on learning generally

Benassi, V. A., Overson, C. E., & Hakala, C. M. (Editors). (2014). Applying science of learning in education: Infusing psychological science into the curriculum. Retrieved from the Society for the Teaching of Psychology website: http://teachpsych.org/ebooks/asle2014/index.php

 —Here's an amazing free resource with chapters summarizing much of the current research on learning with many chapters written by those doing the research and with suggestions for implementing what the research has established.

 If you don't have time to get through a 300-page book, then how about one chapter? Stephen Chew's chapter, "How to Help Students Get the Most out of Studying," is the one not to miss. He starts with the mistaken assumptions students make about studying and moves from there to a succinct discussion of what teachers can do to promote the use of good study strategies.

Halpern, D. F, and Hakel, M. D. (2008). Applying the science of learning to the university and beyond: Teaching for long-term retention and transfer. *Change,* July/August, 36-41.

 —This well organized and clearly written article identifies 10 research-based learning principles that enhance long-term retention and transfer.

How do students study?

Blaisman, R. N., Dunlosky, J., and Rawson, K. A. (2017). The what, how much, and when of study strategies: comparing intended versus actual study behavior. *Memory*, 25 (6), 784-792. [Study Strategies Resource Collection: Study with Practical Implications.]

—Researchers were interested in *what* specific strategies students use to learn, understand and remember course content, *how much* time students spend studying, and *when*, as in what times during the course, do they study. "Our results indicate that during the semester, students rely on relatively ineffective strategies and mass their studying the day or two before an exam." (p. 784)

Hora, M. T. and Oleson, A. K. (2017). Examining study habits in undergraduate STEM courses from a situative perspective. *International Journal of STEM Education, 4* (1), 19 pages [*The Teaching Professor* October, 2017]

—Students in undergraduate science courses were asked to describe in as much detail as possible how they studied in this course. The researchers found that studying was not "easily distilled into a set of discrete strategies" (p. 6/19) but was a multi-faceted process. They also found that these students persisted in using "low-impact" strategies such as re-reading.

Sebesta A. J. and Speth, E. B. (2017). How should I study for the exam? Self-regulated learning strategies and achievement in introductory biology. *Cell Biology Education—Life Sciences Education, 16* (2), 1-12. [*The Teaching Professor* October, 2017]

—Students in an introductory science course were asked what self-regulated study strategies they used. Researcher then looked which of those were associated with higher achievement and how students proposed to study for future exams. They found students had "limited knowledge" of self-regulated strategies and a limited ability to implement them.

Which study strategies does the research say are most effective?

Dunlosky, J., Rawson, K. A., Marsh, E. J., Nathan, M. J. and Willingham, D. T., (2013). Improving student's learning with effective learning techniques: Promising directions from cognitive and educational psychology. *Psychological Science in the Public Interest, 14* (1), 4-58. [*The Teaching Professor* January 2016]

—This lengthy, but very well-organized article, authored by an impressive collection of cognitive psychologists, reviews research on 10 study strategies. Study strategies rated "high" included distributed practice (the opposite of cramming) and practice testing. Interleaved (mixed up) practice, elaborative interrogations and self-explanation were rated as "moderate", and among those strategies given low ratings were highlighting and re-reading, two of students' favorite strategies.

How much do students and faculty know about evidence-based study strategies?

Hunter, A. S., and Lloyd, M. E. (2018). Faculty discuss study strategies, but not the best ones: A survey of suggested exam preparation techniques for difficult courses across disciplines. *Scholarship of Teaching and Learning in Psychology, 4* (2), 105-114.

—123 faculty across a range of disciplines were asked to think of the most difficult course they teach and then share what information they gave to students about how to study. Ninety-one percent study information. However, over 50 percent recommended passive study strategies like re-reading and reviewing. "There is great room for improvement in the information being delivered in college classrooms regarding exam preparation." (p.110)

McCabe, J. (2011). Metacognitive awareness of learning strategies. *Memory and Cognition, 39* (3), 462-476.

—"This research suggests that undergraduates were largely unaware of several specific strategies that could benefit memory for course information." (p. 462)

Morehead, K., Rhodes, M. G., and DeLozier, S. (2016). Instructor and student knowledge of study strategies. *Memory, 24* (2), 257-271. [for a version of the scenarios used in this research see the Study Strategies Resource Collection.]

—On the bases of responses to survey questions and scenarios, these researchers conclude, "Our results suggest that instructors and students have modest knowledge of optimal study strategies and differ little in this regard." (p. 268)

Are there approaches that get students using more effective study strategies?

Chen, P., Chavez, O., Ong, D. C., and Gunderson, B. (2017). Strategic resource use for learning: A self-administered intervention that guides self-reflection on effective resource use enhances academic performance. *Psychological Science, 28* (6), 774-785.

—Prior to exams in a statistics course, students were given a list of 15 study resources, asked which ones they planned to use, why they thought those were useful, and how they planned to use them. Students who experienced this treatment reported "being more self-reflective about their learning throughout the class, used their resources more effectively, and outperformed students in the control condition by an average of one third of a letter grade in the class." (p. 774)

Dang, N., Chiang, J., Brown, H., and McDonald, K. (2018). Curricular activities that promote cognitive skills impact lower-performing students in an introductory biology course. *Journal of Microbiology and Biology Education, 19* (1), 1-9.

—Three curricular interventions were used to promote metacognitive skills development in an introductory biology course. Students completed pre-lecture assignments, participated in collaborative group work (discussions and group quizzes), and an exam review assignment in which students corrected missed questions, diagnosed reasons for their mistakes, and explored their study strategies. "Our findings suggest that assignments designed to promote metacognition can have an impact on students over the course of one semester and may provide the greatest benefits to lower-performing students." (p. 1/9)

A sampling of the evidence supporting individual strategies shown to improve performance and promote learning

Study Groups

McCabe, J. A. and Lummis, S. N. (2018). Why and how do undergraduates study in groups? *Scholarships of Teaching and Learning in Psychology, 4* (1), 27-42. [*The Teaching Professor* Blog, May 2018]

—In a cross disciplinary cohort of 463 students at 38 different institutions, 78 percent said they participated in at least one study group per semester. The top three study strategies students reported using in these groups were asking each other questions, discussing course materials and quizzing each other, all of which are evidence-based strategies. Over 60percent said their level of learning in study groups was somewhat more or a lot more than when studying individually. Almost 70 percent said that study groups increased their motivation to study.

Test Enhanced Learning

Brame, C. J. and Biel, R. (2015). Test-enhanced learning: The potential for testing to promote greater learning in undergraduate science courses. *Cell Biology Education—Life Sciences Education, 14* (Summer), 1-12. [*The Teaching Professor* October 2015]

—These authors identify six benefits that accrue when student "test" themselves on course materials including repeated retrieval practice, needing to find the correct answer and overall improved approaches to study.

Batsell Jr., W. R., Perry, J. L., Hanley, E., and Hostetter, A. B., (2017). Ecological validity of the testing effect: The use of daily quizzes in introductory psychology. *Teaching of Psychology, 44* (1), 18-23. [*The Teaching Professor* February 2017]

—Regular quizzes show the same benefits as self-testing. In this study students in the experimental section had the same content and reading assignments plus a graded quiz every class session. The control and experimental sections each took three exams. Some of those questions were the same questions used on the quiz, some were similar, and some were entirely new questions. The quiz section "scores were significantly higher than the control class" (p. 21) and they were higher on all three types of questions.

Distributed Practice

Benjamin, A. S. and Tullis, J. (2010). What makes distributed practice effective? *Cognitive Psychology, 61* (3), 229-228.

—"The effects of distributing practice are extremely robust and cross-cutting. The advantages are evident in basic memory tasks using words and pictures, in motor skill acquisition and with more complex educationally relevant materials." (pp. 228-229)

Interleaving

Blasiman, R. N., (2017). Distributed concept reviews improve exam performance. *Teaching of Psychology, 44* (1), 46-50.

—A straightforward review technique used in introductory psychology course sections combined both interleaving and distributed practice. Every class session started with a five- to ten-minute review that included key concepts covered in the previous class session and randomly selected material from earlier sessions. Students explained the concepts with the teacher correcting and elaborating their responses as needed. This application of interleaving and distributed practice resulted in students in the experimental sections performing eight percent better on the final exam.

Rohrer, D. (2012). Interleaving helps students distinguish among similar concepts. *Educational Psychology Review, 24* (3), 355-367.

—"In a number of experiments that have compared interleaving [mixing up what's being studied] and blocking [study only similar items], interleaving produced better scores on final tests of learning. The evidence is limited, though, and ecologically valid studies are needed. Still, a prudent reading of the data suggests that at least a portion of the exposures should be interleaved." (p. 355)

Confronting the Myth of Multitasking: A Collection of Tools and Resources

Most of us need no research evidence to document that students are using their phones and attempting to multitask in class. We see it all the time, and if you suspect it's also happening when they study, research confirms that as well. In some ways, we can't really blame students. People are on their phones everywhere, including places where cell phones are supposed to be off. And let's be honest, faculty are pretty much like everyone else when it comes to paying attention to what's on their phone when they shouldn't be—in faculty meetings, workshops, while listening to the college president, and when they grade student work. Students do have a problem, but so does pretty much everyone else. We need big societal changes and those aren't yet forthcoming. Without them, is it any surprise that solutions tried in the classroom have had limited success?

Most faculty have responded to students' proclivity to multitask with policies that prohibit the use of devices in class, significantly curtail their use, or put instructors in charge of when and for what they can be used. (See "Cell Phone Policies: A Review of Where Faculty Stand," *Faculty Focus* March 6, 2018) A growing body of evidence documents how students are responding to these policies. If the class has more than 100 students in it, 90 percent of students reported on one survey that they could text without the instructor knowing (Tindell and Bohlander, 2012). In a study involving smaller class sizes, 32 percent said they could text without the instructor knowing Clayson and Haley, 2013). In the same study, which involved multiple sections of a marketing course, 56 percent of students said that texting in the class was banned and 49 percent said they texted anyway. Whether students can text without us knowing is not as important as the fact students think they can do it without us knowing.

Students are also using their devices when they study. In one study that analyzed student activities in 3,372 computer logs of study sessions, multitasking happened in 70 percent of those sessions (Judd, 2013). Studies referenced in the resources that follow document how frequently students switch between studying and their devices when they study.

As the resources illustrate, this kind of task-switching slows them down and compromises their attempt to learn the material. The amount of notes they take, quiz scores, exam scores even course grades are all negatively affected. Because it's our job to guide, manage, and otherwise direct their learning experiences, we must explore a range of approaches to help make students more acutely aware of how their attempts to learn are being compromised by these devices.

On page 23, you will find a set of questions for students, which they can answer online or in class. They answer for themselves, not for the teacher, other classmates, or anybody else. After they've answered the questions, they get a copy of what research has to say about those questions. The research answers provided are brief, accurate portrayals of the findings, and they're written in way that students will understand the implications. Most of the research on multitasking is complex, complicated, and written primarily to inform subsequent inquiry in this area.

You are welcome to use and adapt these materials. The objective is to confront students' beliefs about multitasking with the evidence. Will that change their behavior? Hopefully it will, but if it doesn't at least students will be attempting to multitask while fully aware that there are consequences.

REFERENCES

Clayson, D. and Haley, D. (2013). An introduction to multitasking and texting: Prevalence and impact on grades and GPA in marketing classes. *Journal of Marketing Education, 35* (1), 26-40.

Judd, T. (2013). Making sense of multitasking: Key behaviours. *Computers & Education, 63*, 358-367.

Tindell, D. R. and Bohlander, R. W. (2012). The use and abuse of cell phones and text messaging in the classroom: A survey of college students. *College Teaching, 60*, 1-9.

MULTITASKING: A SELF-CHECK QUIZ FOR STUDENTS

Instructions: Take a few minutes and jot down your honest answers to the questions below. These answers won't be collected or reviewed, so there's no reason to fudge or spin your responses.

Imagine you are studying for an important exam. Answer the following prompts, thinking about a 15-minute time window during your study session.

1. Would you use any of your devices during that 15 minutes for purposes other than studying?

2. Which one(s) and for how long?

3. How long would you study before using one of your devices?

4. Does switching tasks during study time have any consequences?

3. If so, what are they?

Imagine you're in class, it's a challenging course and one of the first in your major. The professor is lecturing. He/she uses PowerPoint slides but does not make them available to students. A significant portion of the test questions comes from material that is covered in class.

1. Would you be taking notes? By hand or on a laptop or tablet?

2. Would you have your phone with you? Would it be on?

3. If you received a text in this class, would you look at it?

4. Would you answer it?

5. Imagine you are taking in a course where you are tested on the required reading assignments.

Does using devices (e.g. phone, iPad, laptop) slow you down when you're reading assigned material?

If so, how much?

General Questions

1. Have you ever kept track of how much time you're on your devices while studying or in class?

2. Can you listen, take notes, and be on your device simultaneously? In other words, how good are you at multi-tasking?

3. Does multitasking in class lower, raise, or have no effect on quiz and/or exam scores?

4. Does regularly multitasking in a course affect your grade in the course?

MULTITASKING: A LOOK AT SOME OF THE RESEARCH

Now that you've taken the self-check quiz, here's what some research studies have found regarding the efficacy of multitasking in class and while studying.

A note about the evidence presented here—these studies are examples. The widespread use of electronic devices has resulted in much research on multitasking in general and specifically on its use in classrooms and when students study on their own. Even though the studies do ask different questions and use different designs to answer those question, the findings are amazingly consistent. What's briefly highlighted in each section is corroborated by lots of other studies.

Imagine you are studying for an important exam. Answer the following prompts, thinking about a 15-minute time window during your study session.

Would you use any of your devices during that 15 minutes for purposes other than studying? Which one(s) and for how long?

> In a study where participants were observed for a 15-minute study period, the students were on task 65 percent of the time. The more devices available, the more often students used them. (Rosen, Carrier and Cheever, 2013)

> To observe the actions of 60 undergraduates, each studying alone for three hours, researchers used surveillance cameras and outfitted the students with a head-mounted, point-of-view video cameras and mobile eye trackers. On average the students were distracted by media unrelated to studying 35 times for six seconds or longer during the study session. (Calderwood, Ackerman and Conklin, 2014)

How long would you study, before using one of your devices?

During a 15-minute study period, off-task behavior increased significantly at the 4-5 minute mark with the most off-task behavior at the 10-minute mark. (Rosen, Carrier and Cheever, 2013)

Are there any consequences when you switch tasks during study times? If so, what are they?

When asked about the effects of using devices as they studied, 53.3 percent of the students predicted that doing so would negatively affect their performance; 23.3 percent said there would be no effect on performance and 23.4 percent predicted that using devices as they studied would improve performance. The students who anticipated negative effects were correct. (Calderwood, Green, Joy-Gaba and Moloney, 2016)

Students in introductory psychology courses reported how long they studied for an exam and how many of 23 different social media applications and electronic devices they used during that study time. The researcher divided the students into three groups; low users (0-2 applications and devices); medium users (3–6 applications and devices), and higher users (over 7 applications and devices). Low users scored 4.74 point higher on the exam than high users and that was a statistically significant difference (Patterson, 2017)

Imagine you're in class, it's a challenging course and one of the first in your major. The professor is lecturing. He/she uses PowerPoint slides but does not make them available to students. A significant portion of the test questions comes from material that is covered in class.

Would you be taking notes? By hand or on a laptop or tablet?

In a laboratory study that involved six different classroom environments, students who wrote notes by hand out performed students who took notes on a laptop. (Downs, Tran, McMenemy and Abergaze, 2015)

In a classroom setting where students sat either in a laptop-free zone or a laptop zone, those in the laptop-free zone who were taking notes by hand scored significantly higher on exams than predicted by pre-class academic indicators. Those in the laptop zone performed significantly lower than predicted. (Aguilar-Roca, Williams, and O'Dowd, 2012)

Would you have your phone with you? Would it be turned on?

In a cross disciplinary survey, 95 percent of the students reported bringing their phones to class and 91 percent said their phones were set on vibrate. Only nine percent reported turning their phones off. (Tindell and Bohlander, 2012)

If you received a text in this class, would you look at it? Would you answer it?

Ninety-two percent of 269 students said yes to both questions. Thirty percent said they read and answered texts every class session. (Tindell and Bohlander, 2012)

In two different marketing major courses, 94 percent of the students reported receiving texts while in class and 86 percent said that they'd texted while in class. (Patterson, 2013)

Would you be using your phone, tablet, or laptop for purposes not related to what's happening in class? Taking a peek at Instagram? Viewing a favorite website? Firing off a quick text? For how long would you do this?

In an upper-division management information course, students had "distractive windows" (games, pictures, email, web surfing, etc.) open 42 percent of the time during class. Researchers found they underreported their use of email by 7percent and use of instant messaging by 40 percent (Kraushaar and Novak, 2010).

Imagine you are taking in a course where you are tested on the required reading assignments.

Does using devices slow you down when you're reading assigned material? If so, how much?

Students in a general psychology course read a 3,828-word passage online. The group that texted while they were reading took between 22 and 59 percent longer to finish than students who didn't text or texted before they started reading. And those were the percentages after the time spent texting had been subtracted from the reading times. (Bowman, Levine, Waite, and Dendron, 2010)

General Questions

Have you ever kept track of how much time you're on your devices while studying or in class?

In multiple sections of a management information systems course, researchers found that students had non-course-related software applications open and active 42 percent of the time during class. (Kraushaar, J. M. and Novak, D. C., 2010).

Can you listen, take notes, contribute, and be on your device simultaneously? In other words, can you multitask effectively?

Forty-seven percent of marketing majors reported that they could text and follow a lecture simultaneously. (Clayson and Haley, 2013)

In a study where researchers put students into three groups; 1) those who didn't text, 2) those who texted some, and 3) those who texted a lot. The students who didn't text recorded 33 percent of the details presented in the lecture. Low-texting students had 27 percent of the details and high texters only had 20 percent of the details. (Kuznekoff and Titsworth, 2013).

Does multitasking in class have any negative consequences? For example, does it affect quiz or exam scores? Have you experienced any negative consequences?

In a principles of accounting course where half the students were allowed to text during the lecture and half had their phones off, those with their phones off scored significantly higher on the quiz (Ellis, Daniels and Jauregui, 2010).

In several communication courses, students who did not text scored a full course grade higher on a multiple-choice exam than students who were actively texting. (Kuznekoff and Titsworth, 2013)

In this study, researchers created six different classroom environments; three where students were distracted by social media and three where they weren't. Students in the three environments that involved social media performed worse on a multiple-choice exam that those not using social media. (Downs, Tran, McMenemy and Abegaze, 2015)

Does regularly multitasking in a course affect your grade in the course?

Yes, it does, according a large study that involved 1,839 students. Use of Facebook and texting while studying were negatively associated with overall college GPA. (Junco and Cotton, 2012)

So, here's the bottom line. . .

You weren't a student in any of these studies, so it's unknown how using electronic devices when you study, prepare for an exam, and read assigned materials, affects you and your ability to learn. But how it affects a lot of other students is known and the results are uniformly not good.

If you'd like to see if you're different, an outlier among your peers, try this quick exercise. Take a 15-minute study interval and jot the time when you check your phone, the time when you get back to the books, the time a text comes in and you look at it, etc. That way you won't be kidding yourself about how much time you're studying and how time you spend doing something else. Note where you started reading or working the first homework problem and note where you are when the 15 minutes are over. Now do 15 minutes of studying with all of your devices off and out of reach. How much did you get done? How well do you understand what you've done?

In class, turn your phone off (even just for part of the period) and take notes. Compare that set of notes with a set taken when you were dealing with your phone as you took notes.

Perhaps you know that very old saying, "knowledge is power." And that applies when it comes to knowing if and how multitasking impedes your efforts to learn. You may decide to live with consequences, or you may decide your behavior needs to change. Those are choices you're in charge of making. If you do decide to make some changes, knowledge about the effects of multitasking may provide the motivational power.

REFERENCES

Aguilar-Roca, N. M., Williams, A. E., and O'Dowd, D. K. (2012). The impact of laptop-free zones on student performance and attitudes in large lectures. *Computers & Education, 59*, 1300-1308.

Bowman, L. L., Levine, L. E., Waite, B. M. and Dendron, M. (2010). Can students really multitask? An experimental study of instant messaging while reading. *Computers & Education, 54*, 927-931.

Calderwood, C., Ackerman, P. L., and Conklin (2014). What else do college students "do" while studying? An investigation of multitasking. *Computer & Education, 75*, 19-29.

Calderwood, C., Green, J. D., Joy-Gaba, J. A., Moloney, J. M. (2016). Forecasting errors in student media multitasking during homework completion. *Computers & Education, 94*, 37-48.

Clayson, D. and Haley, D. (2013). An introduction to multitasking and texting: Prevalence and impact on grades and GPA in marketing classes. *Journal of Marketing Education, 35* (1), 26-40.

Downs, E., Tran, A., McMenemy, R., Abegaze, N. (2015). Exam performance and attitudes toward multitasking in six multimedia-multitasking classroom environments. *Computers & Education, 86*, 250-259.

Ellis, Y., Daniels, W. and Jauregui, A. (2010). The effect of multitasking on the grade performance of business students. Research in *Higher Education Journal, 8* http://www.aabri.com/manuscripts/10498.pdf

Junco, R. and Cotton, S. R. (2012). No A 4 U: The relationship between multitasking and academic performance. *Computers & Education, 59*, 505-514.

Kraushaar, J. M. and Novak, D. C. (2010). Examining the effect of student multitasking with laptops during lecture. *Journal of Information Systems Education, 21* (2), 241-251.

Kuznekoff, J. H. and Titsworth, S. (2013). The impact of mobile phone usage on student learning. *Communication Education, 62*, 233-252.

Patterson, M. C., (2017). A naturalistic investigation of media multitasking while studying and the effects on exam performance. *Teaching of Psychology, 44* (1), 51-57.

Rosen, L. D., Carrier, L. M., and Cheever, N. A. (2013). Facebook and texting made me do it: Media-induced task-switching while studying. *Computers in Human Behavior, 29*, 948-958.

Tindell, D. R. and Bohlander, R. W. (2012), The use and abuse of cell phones and text messaging in the classroom: A survey of college students. *College Teaching, 60*, 1-9.

Ask 'Em! How Do You Study?

You have your opinions about how students study (or don't) and what they should (and shouldn't) be doing when they study. Asking them is the best way to confirm, correct, and enlarge your understanding of how your students are actually studying.

This question set focuses on how students are working with your course content, assignments and activities. How are they studying for your course? In Section 6: Studying for Exams, there's a question set focused on exam preparation activities. With a bit of revision, you could frame the questions so that they ask how a student studies across courses.

There are options to consider and decision to make before using them.

- What questions should you ask? These questions touch on a wide range of study behaviors. Which are most relevant given the content and the activities and assignments of the course? Which are of most interest to you? Could you let students identify some of the questions that are of interest to them?

- How do you want students to answer—with closed or open-ended questions? There's a set of each below. Open-ended questions produce a wide range of responses. You use them to look for theme and the occasional great insight. Closed questions produce results you can quantify, calculate averages, standard deviations, etc. The closed statement below can be answered yes/no or used with use a Likert-type scale with numbers or descriptors such as; very often, often, sometimes, rarely, or never. You could add one or two open-ended questions at the end of the closed question set: If you could improve one thing about how you study, what would you improve? What can the teacher do to better support your efforts to study?

- How do you want to collect and analyze the data? Do you want to use a tool such as Survey Monkey or a feature of your local LMS?

- What will you do with the results? Use them to enlarge your understanding of how students study? Share and discuss the results with students, in class or online? Sharing the results with students allows them to benchmark their behavior against their peers in the course. You could collect responses from students doing well in the course and then use those results in subsequent courses so that students have accurate information as how much and what kind of study it takes to do well in the course.

- Will you make changes based on the results? If so, what will you change and how? If students identify some teacher actions that would better support their efforts to learn, and you provide some of those, research indicates that's very motivating to students. So if they asked for an in-class review session before the exam and you provide it, they would likely show up and be ready to review.

HOW DO YOU STUDY?

A NOTE FROM YOUR TEACHER

I'm interested in learning more about how you're studying in this course. My goal is to teach in ways that support your efforts to study, that help you learn the material, and do well on the exams. I can do that better if I'm not guessing about how you study or making decisions on false assumptions. So please be honest. The goal here is not to impress me with how much you're studying but to help me understand how you're working to learn the material in this course. Thanks for taking the time to answer these questions. I will be sharing results with the class and talking about what I've learned.

OPEN-ENDED QUESTIONS ABOUT STUDYING IN THIS COURSE

1. If the goal is getting an A in this course, how much time would a student need to devote to the course on a weekly basis?

2. Describe your study activities for course during the last five days.

3. When you're studying and you discover something you really don't understand, what do you do?

4. Do you multi-task (check your various devices) when you're studying in this course? If so, what else are you doing while you are studying?

5. What study strategies are working best for you in this course?

6. Do you study as much as you should for this course? If so, what prevents you from studying more?

7. Are there any instructional strategies being used in the course that help you learn the material?

8. Are there any instructional strategies or features of the course that make it difficult to understand the content?

9. How motivated are you to study in this course, compared with other courses you've taken?

10. How confident are that the ways you study and prepare in this course will improve your performance in the course?

11. What specific study strategies are you finding work best for you in this course?

12. Is there something about the way you are studying for this course that you'd like to improve?

CLOSED QUESTIONS ABOUT STUDYING IN THIS COURSE

Answer with very often, often, sometimes, rarely, or never

1. If you want to get an A on an exam in this course, you would need to study 20 hours or more.

2. While studying, you may listen to music, check social media, text, snack and take calls.

3. During the past five days, you have studied for this course 10 hours.

4. You take notes in class and use them when you study.

5. You go to class having done the assigned readings.

6. When you are confused or not understanding content in the course, you talk to the professor after class or during office hours.

7. You study with others when reviewing material in the course.

8. You study alone.

9. The study skills you are developing now will be used in your chosen career.

10. You are motivated to improve your use of study strategies in this course.

11. The instructional strategies used in the course support your efforts to study.

12. I do my best work on the assignments for this course.

13. I meet the assignment due dates and deadlines.

Advice on How to Study: Who Should Give It?

Teachers typically offer students lots of advice on how to study. It's delivered verbally in class before and after exams, in online communications, on the syllabus, and in the office, especially when teachers meet with students who aren't doing well in the course. Do students listen to and heed that advice? Not as regularly as we might like.

In physics course I was observing, at the end of the session the teacher announced that the class was having a test next week and that he had a handout with some advice on how to study for the exam. Students went about packing up and preparing to leave. But I noticed as soon as the handout was received, the packing up stopped. Book bags went back down, students were reading the handout.

When a copy came to me, I saw why. The handout contained study recommendations from students who had taken the class previously. They were identified by name as was the grade they'd received in the class.

And what advice did these students offer? "Come to class regularly. He goes over problems in class very much like ones that show up on the exam." "Don't wait until the night before the exam to start doing the homework problems. Make it a habit to do problems every week." "If you don't understand something, ask about it. Chances are good you aren't the only one who doesn't understand." "It helps to check homework with somebody else in class, not to copy answers, but to see how somebody else did the problem." Students gave the very same advice I'd heard countless professors offer, but I'd never seen students attending to teacher advice this seriously.

Sometime after I was in this class, the prof told me that he'd started putting advice on the sheet from students who had struggled in the class. Many of them wrote candidly about things they'd done that didn't work. They described things they should have done but didn't how those inactions hurt their grade.

Resources in this section make clear that students don't always use the best study strategies, so that is a caveat. And I'm not suggesting that teachers stop offering advice. We have, after all, studied this content more than our students. But a student who's just taken the course has a kind of credibility we can't match.

In the example, the student advice is about how to study for an exam. It could easily be advice on how to do the big term project or more generally advice on how to succeed in the course. Now it could be share online, in an electronic communique or maybe a podcast discussion among a panel of students.

REVIEW AND REFLECTION

WORKSHEET 1

Yes, it's a worksheet, yes, there are two of them and no, you don't have to do either of them. They're included here and after every chapter to encourage you to pause and reconsider what you've just looked at in light of your current practice. They also confront you with the change question: should you take action based on these resources? If so, what's here that you could use? What actions do you need to take?

1. What firsthand, factual knowledge do you have about how your students study for the courses you teach?

2. How well is your policy regarding use of electronic devices in class working? What percentage of your students believe they can multi-task with few if any consequences? What are you doing to disavow them of this faulty assumption?

3. Say you tell students that you've been looking at some materials on study strategies. What would you tell them you've learned?

4. Are there ways of studying that are particularly important to learning the content you teach? Can you describe them? Are those the skills you need to be emphasizing in your courses?

5. Can you show students that there are better ways of studying rather than just telling them?

REFLECTION, ACTION, AND RESULTS

WORKSHEET 2

REFLECTION

Resources in the section made me think about these points differently, or, my biggest take away from this section was...

ACTION

❑ I plan to use the How Do You Study tool in this chapter to gain firsthand, factual knowledge about how my students study for the courses I teach.

❑ I plan to revisit my policy on electronic devices to create a more compelling rationale to help my students stop multitasking in class and during study time. I will have a revised policy in place by next semester.

❑ I am going to show-not-tell my students about study strategies in these three ways:

1. _____

2. _____

3. _____

RESULTS

Here's my plan for assessing the actions I'm planning to take:

After taking those actions, I've seen these differences in my students, their learning and my teaching:

Instructional Strategies that Develop Study Skills

Introduction

With content packed courses, most of us don't have a lot of time to devote to working with students on their study skills. What we can do is illustrate good study habits by embedding them in our instructional practices. We can make the pitch to students that these are the very approaches research has shown improve performance in courses and yes, that means higher exam scores.

Resources in this section illustrate some the many approaches teachers can take. For example, the regular in-course use of reviews and summaries showcases research findings on distributed practice. Regular and frequent interactions with content, even short ones, trump cramming with improved exam scores and long-term retention. The problem is that most of the time, it's the teacher who does the reviews and summaries. Students can benefit from listening to a succinct, well-organized review but not nearly as much as they benefit from doing the summary themselves. Will their summaries be as good as those offered by the teacher? Probably not in the beginning. But learning to review and summarize is a skill that serves students well in their courses and beyond.

Big assignments in most courses require execution of skills students may not have or have had the opportunity to practice. Low-stakes assignments can be designed to provide the opportunity to practice skills. Mistakes on these assignments count less which makes them less traumatic. In many cases it's the process of doing the low-stakes assignment that garners the learning benefits and that means they don't have to be assignments that require extensive teacher feedback.

Quizzes are another excellent activity when it comes to reinforcing good study habits. They make frequent, interaction with the content a necessity if students want to earn high quiz scores. They encourage students to come to class prepared which makes what happens in class more meaningful. A missed quiz question confronts students with something about the content that they don't understood or hasn't been learned yet. One of the resources included in this section highlights research-identified benefits associated with the use of quizzes. The extent to which those benefits are realized does depend in part on the careful design of quizzes and there's some interesting options also in the materials that follow.

Similar points can be made about in-class review sessions scheduled before exams and the debrief sessions that occur after them. Rather being a time when the teacher "goes over" the content, often working harder than the students, these sessions can be filled with activities that get students engaged with the content in ways that showcase effective exam preparation activities and how learning that didn't happen for the exam can still occur after it. There's a list of those activities for both review and debrief sessions in this section. Many of them can be adapted for use online.

When it comes to those big exam and assignment events, there will be students disappointed in their grades. Most don't talk to the teacher even though it's a chance for more feedback and good advice about preparing the next event. The resource explains why students don't talk about disappointing grades and most of the reasons are things teachers can do something about.

Learning the content and developing the skills that add efficiency and effectiveness to learning the content are both tasks that only students can do. Teachers can help with the motivation and they can include learning experiences that provide the know-how and showcase the benefits.

Regular, Ongoing, In-class Review

Don't underestimate the value of regular in-class review. Most of us already spend time doing it, but usually we're the ones doing all the work. What's different about these strategies is that they get students doing the reviewing. They model evidence-based study strategies—ones that improve exam performance. The hope is that regular use of strategies like this will showcase their value to students.

- **Use test questions—students pay attention to them.** They might be questions you've used before or questions you might possibly use. Find more ideas on using test questions in Section 6: Studying for Exams.

  - ☐ Have one question displayed at the beginning of the session. "Here's a test question I've asked about the material covered when we were last together." Encourage students to test themselves. Let them talk to each other. Have them look in their notes to see if they have material there that helps them answer the question. Unanswered questions keep students engaged and attentive longer than those that are answered directly, especially if several possible answers are proposed.

  - ☐ Have students create a potential test question at the end of the period or online lesson. Ask students to take a look at their notes. "This material is fair game for the exam. What might a test question on this material ask? How about jotting down some ideas?" Then ask several students share their ideas. Identify those you think could be good exam questions. If you use one of their suggested questions on the test, that pretty much guarantees they'll take this activity seriously. It's also a great way to get students reviewing their notes and discovering what they do and don't have in them. And there's an added benefit: what students suggest as possible question gives you feedback as to what they think is important.

- **Regularly (as in at least once a session) ask or embed questions about previously covered material**

  - ☐ Resolutely refuse to answer the question. That's exactly students want you to do.

  - ☐ Give them a hint. "We talked about this when we were talking about X." "Check your notes for October 20. You might find the answer there."

  - ☐ Be patient. It takes time for students to retrieve what they've just learned and barely understand.

  - ☐ Still no response? Tell them, that's the question you'll start with tomorrow and if they don't have an answer then, they'll next see that question on the exam.

- **Get students doing short reviews.** They can open the session, occur during class when students need a break, or they can be a summary activity.

  □ "Let's all look at our notes from March 3. You've got two minutes to underline the three things in your notes that you're going to need to review for the exam." Ask several what they've underlined and why. An activity like this can make students who don't have notes for the day nervous and uncomfortable which is precisely how they should feel.

  □ "Take three minutes to review your notes from November 1. Do you have anything in your notes that doesn't make sense to you now? Share what that is." Encourage other students to respond to what's not making sense now. "Help Shandra out. What do you the rest of you have in your notes about this? Is there something in the text that clarifies this?" Conclude by giving them another minute to write more in their notes if they need to.

  □ Here's a great strategy proposed by Annie Blazer. She assigns students (one per day) to open class with a 3–5-minute review of the material presented in the previous class session. In addition to getting students reviewing, this strategy gives students practice doing a presentation in class. It helps them learn how to summarize. And finally, you can imagine the kind of careful note taking that occurs the day before a student is scheduled to present. (For more information see: Blazer, A. (2014). Student summaries of class sessions. *Teaching Theology and Religion, 17* (4), 344.)

Quizzes: What They Do and Don't Accomplish

In terms of outcomes related to learning, the case for using quizzes is strong. Studies document the following results:

- they get students coming to class (and on time, if the quiz is what begins class)

- students report spending more time reading when quizzes are a part of the course than in sections of the same course where there are no quizzes

- students report spending more time studying between exams when the course has quizzes (i.e. less cramming and more regular studying, i.e. distributed practice)

- students report that a quiz or the possibility of one motivates them to come to class prepared

- they're practice tests and derive the benefits of test-enhanced learning if the grading stakes are low

- they increase participation in courses

- they lower failure rates in courses

- they improve scores on mid-course tests and on the final: with quizzes on assigned readings the improvement in exam scores is between two and five percent (see Pape-Lindstrom, et.al. for references)

- online quizzing where students were allowed to use books and notes still resulted in improved exam scores

- they improve overall course grades

- using quizzes does not lower course or instructor evaluations

REFERENCES

Research on quizzing is extensive, so what's below is a small sample of studies reporting one or more of these benefits.

Azorlosa, J. W. (2011). The effect of announced quizzes on exam performance: II. *Journal of Instructional Psychology, 38*, 3-7

Braun, K. W., and Sellers, R. D. (2012). Using a "daily motivational quiz" to increase student preparation, attendance and participation. *Issues in Accounting Education, 27* (1), 267-279.

Hardsell, L. (2009). The effect of quiz timing on exam performance. *Journal of Education for Business, 84* (3), 135-141.

Hatteberg, S. J. and Steffy, K., (2013). Increasing reading compliance of undergraduates: An evaluation of compliance methods. *Teaching Sociology, 41* (4), 346-352.

Johnson, B. C., and Kiviniemi, M. T. (2009). The effect of online chapter quizzes on exam performance in an undergraduate social psychology course. *Teaching of Psychology, 36* (1), 33-37.

Kouyoumdjian, H. (2004). Influence of unannounced quizzes and cumulative final on attendance and study behavior. *Teaching of Psychology, 31* (2), 110-111.

Pape- Lindstron, Eddy, S., and Freeman, S. (2018). Reading quizzes improve exam scores for community college students. *CBE—Life Sciences Education, 17* (2), 8 pp.

In terms of outcomes related to teaching, quizzes are almost always more work for the teacher although some design features and technology can make the workload manageable.

The case against using quizzes rests on these reasons:

- To make the workload manageable, many teachers use short, ease to score questions: most of them test recall, they encourage students to memorize details, they don't test understanding, and what's memorized for the quiz tends to be quickly forgotten. Quiz questions create expectations for exam questions, thereby influencing how students study for exams.

- Who wants to deal with the logistics? Students arrive late, wanting to do the quiz even though the rest of the class has completed it. Students want to take the quiz beforehand because they're leaving on a university sanctioned activity. Students miss quizzes for what sound like legitimate reasons. Students do terribly on a quiz for what sound like legitimate reasons.

- Not all the research on quizzing reports improved test scores. Here's a study (and it's not the only one) showing that result.

  Haveryan, K. A. (February 2003). Do weekly quizzes improve student performance on general biology exams? *The American Biology Teacher, 65* (2), 110-114.

- Quizzes derive their effectiveness from extrinsic motivation. Students aren't preparing for quizzes they want to or because they understand the value of coming to class having done the reading or homework problems. Instead students prep for class because they may be having a quiz. Intrinsically motivated students do the reading and the problems because they know that coming to class prepared makes what happens in class more meaningful. How often do students who are studying for the quiz understand that the real reason is coming to class prepared?

Quizzes: Creative Alternatives

Sometimes we get stuck in a rut. We administer a short quiz at the beginning of the session. It gets students arriving on time and their answers to the objective questions make clear who's prepared. But this isn't the only option. Here are nine creative alternatives, most described in greater detail in the reference that follows the description.

Mix up the structure—Elizabeth Tropman makes a strong case for reading quizzes. She changes the quiz structure on a regular basis. Sometimes it's the usual objective questions, other times it's short-answer questions, or it might be a question that asks for an opinion response to the reading. Some quizzes are open-book; a few are take home. What an interesting way to give students experience responding to different kinds of test questions and to keep quiz experiences from becoming stale.

REFERENCE

Tropman, E., (2014). In defense of reading quizzes. *International Journal of Teaching and Learning in Higher Education, 26* (1), 140-146.

Collaborative quizzing—Lots of different options are being used here. Students do the quiz, turn it over, stand up and talk with a partner, to others in a small group, or with whomever they choose. After the discussion, they return to their quiz and may change any of their answers. Alternatively, students do the quiz individually, turn it in, and then do the same quiz in a small group. The two quiz scores are combined with the individual score counting for 75 percent of the grade and the group quiz 25 percent (or some other weighted variation). Collaborative quizzing is an effective way to generate enthusiastic discussion of course content and reduce test anxiety.

REFERENCE

Pandey, C., and Kapitanoff, S. "The Influence of Anxiety and Quality of Interaction on Collaborative Test Performance." *Active Learning in Higher Education*, 2011, 12 (3), 163-174.

Quizzing with resources—Students take detailed notes on the reading because they're allowed to use those notes during the quiz. The same approach works with quizzes that cover content presented during class. Students may use their class notes while taking the quizzes. The pay-off is a good (or better) set of notes for use during exam preparation. Ali Resaei reports that open-note quizzing coupled with collaboration resulted in significantly higher final exam scores in his quantitative research methods course.

REFERENCE

Rezaei, A. R., (2015). Frequent collaborative quiz taking and conceptual learning. *Active Learning in Higher Education, 16* (3), 187-196.

Quizzing after questioning—Before the quiz occurs, give students the opportunity to ask questions about potential quiz content. The instructor and the class work on finding the right answer or discussing the merits of possible responses. If someone asks a question that stimulates a lot of good discussion, that question becomes the quiz question and students have the designated amount of time to write an answer. Or if a variety of good questions have been asked, answered, and discussed by a variety of students, you may tell students they've just had their quiz and everyone present gets full credit. This approach encourages students to ask better questions and facilitates substantive classroom discussions.

"Community Space" quiz support—Audrey Deterding came up with this alternative "to inspire the often-dull quiz routine." At the beginning of the class, two randomly selected students have three minutes to write anything from assigned materials on the chalk/white board which become a "community space." Students may use anything that's been written there during the quiz. The two students may collaborate with each other during the three minutes; the rest of the class remains silent. A student selected to write may decline, but a replacement will not be chosen. "The expectation that they [students] may have to share information in the community space motivates most students to closely read the assigned materials. They want to help their classmates perform well on the quizzes and they don't want to appear lazy or irresponsible to their peers." She also reports that the approach encourages collaborative learning and creates a sense of community in the class.

REFERENCE

Deterding, A. L., (2010). A new kind of "space for quizzes. *The Teaching Professor*, November, p. 3.

Online quizzes completed before class—Students complete an online quiz before class. The quizzes are graded electronically with a compiled summary going to the professor so there's enough time to look at the most frequently missed problems and/or to identify areas of misunderstanding. Then class time can be used to address those concepts that are giving students the most trouble.

REFERENCE

Drinkwater, M. J., Gannaway, D., Sheppard, K., Davis, M. J., Wegener, M. J., Bowen, W. P., and Corney, J. F., (2014). Managing active learning processes in large first year physics classes. *Teaching and Learning Inquiry, 2* (2), 75-90.

A way to make up a missed question—It's the standard daily quiz format; three conceptual questions answered during the first five minutes of class. No make-ups are allowed but the three lowest scores are dropped and one missed quiz question per day can be made up by voluntarily participating during class discussions. This is one of several motivational features of this quiz design.

REFERENCE

Braun, K. W. and Sellers, R. D., (2012). Using a 'daily motivational quiz' to increase student preparation, attendance and participation. *Issues in Accounting Education, 27* (1), 267-279.

A take home quiz that promotes discussion—This quiz consists of five questions and is assigned several days before a designated course topic will be discussed in class. Students find and provide a link to a recent article or video on the topic. The remainder of the questions encourage thinking and application of course content to the topic students have selected. Patricia Stan reports, "Being able to pick topics of interest motivates students. Our discussion are informal and lively. I have found this approach reduces the fear of giving a wrong answer in front of the class so more students participate. These discussions help me understand how those outside chemistry view it."

REFERENCE

Stan, P. L. (2015). A quiz that promotes discussion and active learning in large classes. *The Teaching Professor*, March.

The "Unquiz"—Janet Starks passes out a quiz and students groan. Then she tells them to find a partner and do the quiz together. They may use their notes. The quizzes are corrected in class but not collected or graded. She reports students tackled the quiz with enthusiasm—65 percent of them reported on a survey that it helped them learn. She now uses it as a regular review strategy in church history courses.

REFERENCE

Stark, J. (2015). The Unquiz. *The Teaching Professor*, March.

Low-Stakes Assignments: Challenges and Opportunities

Low-stakes assignments include work we have students do that doesn't count for a large part of the course grade. There's a strong set of reasons to use these kinds of assignments, but also some challenges. Let's take stock.

Opportunities from low-stakes assignments

Low-stakes assignments provide opportunities to practice using the skills and knowledge needed to complete the large projects in a course; be those high-stakes exams, major writing assignments, or other complex projects done individually or in groups. This benefit accrues only if the low-stakes tasks involve skills or work with content similar to that required by the big assignments. Quiz questions reinforce content knowledge and can get students comfortable with the kinds of test questions they face in the course. Short analysis papers can give student practice constructing the arguments they'll need to put together for the longer position paper. Impromptu discussion can prepare students for more formal presentations.

Low-stakes assignments significantly diminish the pressure to always get a good grade. When there's only a few chances to earn points, students get stressed and that often compromises their ability to do their best work. Or, they become fixated on doing exactly what they think the teacher wants. In both cases, what they might be learning by doing the assignment takes a back seat. Low-stakes assignments tend to be more learning focused than grade focused.

Low-stakes assignments allow students to fail when the consequences aren't dire. We learn from mistakes, often in profound and memorable ways. But most of our students live in fear of making mistakes. They don't take risks, or try things they don't know how to do, or don't think they can do. To them, education and learning are not the grand adventures we know them to be. Low-stakes assignments put course work in a safer context.

Low-stakes assignments can reinforce good study habits. Most of these assignments (quizzes and reaction papers, for example) provide ongoing, regular interaction with the content. Students (and some of the rest of us) tend to procrastinate. If they stay up all night writing a paper, preparing for an exam, or doing a project they had weeks to complete, they never experience the improved performance that results from working regularly on or in preparation for the big course assessments.

Low-stakes assignments are an efficient way to develop skills that are not the main focus of the course but important across the curriculum. Students could write in a math course; craft arguments in an engineering course; or work in groups in a poetry course. Low-stakes assignments imply short experiences using the skills but collectively those experiences reinforce the pervasiveness of the skill.

The challenges of low-stakes assignments (and some solutions)

Students don't take low-stakes assignments seriously. They don't count for much so they can be written off and some (or is it a lot of) students notoriously underestimate how much can be written off without serious consequences. When it's early in the semester several can be skipped because there's lots more to come, or they can be ignored because the exams count for so much more. If written off, then none of the assignments' potential is realized.

Solution: Explain the rationale behind these assignments. Let there be some serious consequences if they aren't collectively taken seriously. For example, a set of quiz scores well below average might mandate an extra exam.

To students, low-stakes assignments look like the busy work that was the bane of their existence in high school. That's not what they expected to have to do in college: worksheets, nightly homework problems, questions on the reading. Bad attitudes about low-stakes assignments also compromise what they can accomplish. These attitudes, coupled with their low point value, encourage students to complete them with the least amount of effort.

Solution: Provide examples that illustrate the level of quality that's expected. Explicitly point out the connections between the low- and high-stakes assignments.

These brief assignments generate an endless stream of assignments that must be graded, and grading is already a least favorite aspect of teaching activity.

Solution: Devise efficient grading processes. Don't provide a lot of individual feedback. Give the class feedback with anonymous examples. Use a rubric. Collect them all but randomly select a subset and grade those.

Exam Review Sessions

Do you spend class time reviewing before exams? Students are definitely in favor of those sessions. Their goals are straightforward: find out as much as they can about what's going to be on the test. The typical review session helps students accomplish this goal. They can ask the teacher questions, identify problems they'd like the teacher to solve, or query about what's important in the readings. In too many review sessions, the teacher is working way harder than the students. And is it the teacher who needs to review the material?

Some teachers don't like to give up class time to essentially go over material they've already covered. Trying to find a time outside of class that that works for everyone can be challenging. Then there's the issue of who shows up for the review session. Usually it's not the students who most need to be there. Technology does make reviewing online possible, but many teachers still question the legitimacy of exam review sessions.

Biology professor Terence Favero makes a strong case for devoting class time to exam reviews. "Like many teachers, I fought against trading 'content' or course time for an entire class period devoted to a review session. Over time, I came to the conclusion that if I wanted my students to become problem-solvers, I had to provide them with low-stakes opportunities and time to solve them. More importantly, I knew I was the students' best resource for exam preparation." (p. 248)

Favero doesn't focus his review sessions on rehashing content. Instead he opts for problem-solving activities. "Because of the vast amount of information in textbooks and other electronic media, most students today have a difficult time discerning the essential content of the discipline and how it might be used to solve problems." (p. 247) To help students discern essential content and how to use it, Favero first uses "open-ended strategy." Students start by writing down the five most important facts, theories, or concepts from the content that will be covered in the exam. They partner and compare lists. Favero then tallies and lists the topics on an overhead transparency. He adds topics students have missed and then arranges the topics in order of their importance. Next, students, working in groups, generate two or three multiple-choice questions for topics on the list. These are presented and answered collectively in class. "Students regularly question each other on confusing language or selection of the answers, again revealing what student know (or don't) and how they know it. Time permitting, we rewrite the questions so they could be exam worthy." (pp. 247-248)

For the second activity Favero brings to class 8–10 questions taken from previous exams. "I typically avoid knowledge or comprehension questions and focus on application-, analysis-, and synthesis-type questions." (p. 248) Favero works hard to get students to outline key concepts and pieces of the problem first. "Too often, I find that student learning short circuits when they attempt to identify the answer without first identifying how to solve the problem." (p. 248) He always includes a "tricky," as in difficult, question, not to frighten students, but to talk them through how to approach challenging problems.

This strategy also means fewer surprises on the exam itself. Students are correctly anticipating the kind of problems they will be asked to solve.

Students don't always embrace these review activities when they first experience them. They are used to reviews where they ask the questions and get answers. These sessions require them to work and shows them how well they are or aren't prepared for the exam. Finally, he notes that these review activities have revealed strengths and weaknesses in his teaching. Sometimes he thinks material presented on a particular topic has been well explained and is understood by students. During the review he finds out that students either didn't understand at all or don't understand correctly. "The review sessions help me identify content areas that needed attention, something that end of the semester evaluations do not." (p. 248)

REFERENCE

Favero, T. G. (2011). Active review sessions can advance student learning. *Advances in Physiology Education, 35* (3), 247-248.

What's going to be on the test?

A faculty member who read Favero's article came up with an interesting version of one of his strategies. It starts with the question students most want answered during a review session: "What's going to be on the exam?" This faculty member tells students (what most of them already know), the vast majority of teachers are going to do their best to not answer that question. "It's a question students need to be able to answer for themselves."

So, students are challenged to quickly look over the material that will be covered in this exam and write down five things they are pretty darn sure they will need to know for the exam. He gives them 3–5 minutes. Next, he tells them to share their lists with two, three, or four students sitting nearby and as a group to come up with seven things everyone agrees they will need to know. Those items are written down and given to the instructor.

Using the students' lists, this teacher compiles (without editing) a list that contains the most commonly mentioned content areas. "Here's what your classmates think you'll need to know for the exam," reads the post he places on the course website. The payoff comes during the exam debrief, when this class list reappears as a PowerPoint slide. The class then marks off items on the list that did in fact end up on the exam. So far, it's been pretty close to 80 percent and what wasn't on the student list makes for good discussion.

The exam debrief session

If you think about a debrief session as one last opportunity for students to learn important content that they didn't know or misunderstood, then debriefs are definitely work the class time they take. The learning that needs to happen during them is much less likely to occur if the teacher is the one who "goes over" the most missed questions. Was the teacher the one who missed those questions? Again, as in class review sessions, it should not be the teacher who's doing most of the work. These sessions need to be designed so that students are confronting content they didn't know or misunderstand.

Exam Debriefs

Brief—that pretty much describes exam debriefs in many courses. The teacher goes over the most commonly missed questions, and the students can ask about answers but generally don't. These kinds of debriefs don't take up a lot of class time, but that's about all that can be said for them. For some time now, I've been suggesting that students, not the teacher, should be correcting the wrong answers. The students are the ones who missed the questions.

As I continue to assemble a collection of resources on the learning potential inherent in testing events, my thinking about how we debrief exams is changing. A debrief can accomplish two important goals. First, it's another opportunity for students to encounter content they haven't yet learned. I know that raises the question of second chances. I don't believe we should excuse students from the consequences of their study decisions, but test scores often reveal the absence of important knowledge or serious misunderstandings. I've decided that I'm willing to concede on the ethics of second chances if there's an opportunity for students to redress content deficiencies.

Second, debriefs are an ideal time for students to confront the efficacy of the approaches they are using to prepare for exams. Exams get students' attention. With their exam scores in front of them, there's an openness to considering how it came to be.

Here are two strategies that illustrate how these goals can be accomplished without requiring extra class time. The March 2016 issue of *The Teaching Professor* newsletter describes a "two-stage testing" process whereby students take the exam and then correct the exam answers. Students can make corrections independently or in collaboration with others, either within class or outside of it. Since reading the article, I've learned about an earlier version of this strategy called "self-correcting" exams. Here's how it worked in Montepare's psychology class. Students took a typical multiple-choice exam. They put their answers on the exam and on a teacher-provided answer sheet. They turned in the answer sheet and took the exam home. They had until the next class period to change their answers. Both the in-class and at-home exams were scored. If the answer was right on both, it counted for two points. If it was right on one but not the other, the student earned one point. And if it was wrong on both, no points were awarded. In her article, Montepare answers a number of questions about the strategy: Can students cheat? Do they? Does this contribute to grade inflation? Do students come to the exam less prepared, knowing they'll have that second chance?

The most important question about this approach is whether it promotes learning. In two subsequent studies, students took two self-correcting exams and one cumulative final, not self-corrected. Francis and Barnett (2012) report a "marginally significant interaction," one they describe as a "relatively poor investment" given the time required to implement the strategy. Gruhn and Cheng (2014) report more positive results with students performing better on the final than those taking the same final but without having had the self-correcting activity. They also confirmed Montepare's observation that the approach benefits low-performing students.

The second strategy encourages students to conduct an exam analysis where they review their exam and look at the questions missed to see if there's a pattern (are they missing questions for the same reason?). Then they write brief descriptions of how they studied and, based on that information, they consider if there are changes that might better prepare them for the next exam. The instructor lists a number of study options and demonstrates a variety of them while teaching. After their analysis, students schedule a short meeting with the professor to discuss what they've learned. Approximately 50 percent of the students in a human anatomy course participated in this exam analysis, and those who did significantly improved their scores on the second exam. The exam debrief protocol students used is included in the article, and a more detailed discussion of the strategy appears in an upcoming issue of the newsletter. (This strategy is described in detail in Section 6: Studying for Exams, Confronting Exam Performance.)

Both of these approaches significantly change exam debrief experiences. Both challenge us to consider how we debrief exams and what we hope to accomplish with our post-exam analysis.

REFERENCES

Montepare, J. M., (2005). A self-correcting approach to multiple-choice tests. *APS Observer, 18* (10), 35-36.

Francis, A. L. and Barnett, J., (2012). The effect and implications of a "self-correcting" assessment procedure. *Teaching of Psychology, 39* (1), 38-41.

Gruhn, D. and Cheng, Y., (2014). A self-correcting approach to multiple-choice exams improves students' learning. *Teaching of Psychology, 41* (4), 335-339.

Favero, T. G. and Hendricks, N., (2016). Student exam analysis (debriefing) promotes positive change in exam preparation and learning. *Advances in Physiology Education, 40* (3), 323-328.

Test Review Session Activities

Here's a set of activities that get students doing the reviewing during a session devoted to test review. I recommend having students work together on these activities in groups of 4–6. It's a way to let them experience the benefits of a study group by being in one that's using good exam review strategies. Most of these activities can also be completed by students working in groups online.

- Assign each group a different section of text material and have them prepare a set of study questions or a study guide for that section. Each group submits their materials and they are posted or distributed so that others in the course can use them.

- Assign each group a chunk of content and have them prepare five test questions or problems on that material. If the questions are prepared electronically, they can be submitted and then shared with the rest of the class. Important reminder: Students need advice on writing good multiple-choice (and other kinds of) questions. Share guidelines and samples of good and not-so-good questions.

- Give each group a set of potential test questions or problems. The group answers without using their books or notes. The questions they've missed are quickly marked. Then the group finds or corrects their answers. If they correct their answer and identify where they found the correct answer, they get half credit. Members of the group with the highest score get one (or several) bonus points added to their exam score. You can justify making the questions challenging because they are working together on the questions. If you do make some of the questions a bit harder than those on the test, that can motivate students to study and it will make the actual exam questions seem easier.

- Give the group a set of short-answer questions and answers. Include answers at various quality levels. Task the group with grading the answers. Have them identify content errors in the answers and make suggestions as to what would improve the answer. End this activity with a whole-class discussion during which the characteristics of good short answers are identified. Then, the characteristics might be transformed into a rubric that students could use to assess answers they may be creating as they prepare for the exam.

- Give groups a set of multiple-choice answer options. The group's task is to write the question (or stem). Note: this is a very challenging activity that easily frustrates students. They get worried that you'll try something like this on the exam. Assure them you won't. The value of the activity is how effectively it focuses students on questions.

- Every person in the group gets a different potential essay question. During a designated amount of time, each group member finds material in notes and the readings that could be used in the answer. Then each group member talks about their question and identifies potential answer material. Here again technology can be used to expedite the exchange of these materials.

- Assign each group several class sessions and using their individual notes, have the group construct a comprehensive set of notes for those class sessions. Their notes are submitted and distributed to the rest of the students as an exam preparation resource. This activity can provide examples of the level of detail needed in order for class notes to be useful review resources.

- Students prep a crib sheet containing course content which they are allowed to use during the exam. This activity could be structured in a number of ways. If students attend the review session, they work in small groups to prepare the crib sheet. They submit it at the end of the session, and it is returned to them attached to their exam. Or, the activity could start with a small group discussion focused on what to put on the card, then students could be given a blank card and a few minutes to make their individual cards which they submit and then find attached to their exam. An activity like this motivates most students to attend the review session and preparing the crib sheet results in some substantive reviewing during the session.

Getting Students to Talk about Those Disappointing Grades

Handing back graded work or posting grade results is not usually a favorite course event for teachers. There are always those students disappointed in their grades. Some simply look disappointed; others quickly switch from disappointment to anger. A few take it up with the teacher after class. Still fewer show up during office hours to talk about the grade. Bottom line: Most students don't talk with their teachers about those grades they don't think they deserve, though they should for their own benefit and the teacher's. Students can get additional feedback that may help them understand the grade and avoid similar mistakes on subsequent assignments. Teachers can learn how students understood the goals of the activity.

Courtney Wright asked 586 students if they'd received a disappointing grade and if they'd discussed it with the teacher. Of that cohort, 261 said yes, they had received a disappointing grade and no, they had not talked with the teacher about it. Wright asked why they had not, in an open-ended question, and received 343 reasons in response. Most of those reasons fell into these six categories.

Utility of the conversation—These students didn't see any benefit coming from having the conversation. It wasn't going to result in the grade being changed. "This narrow focus may cause some students to misjudge the utility of meeting with an instructor, missing out on the many potential benefits afforded from doing so." Reasons in this category were the most often given, counting for 27 percent of all the reasons offered for not talking about the grade with the teacher.

Understanding of the grade causes—In this case students didn't talk with the instructor because they understood the reasons why they got the grade. They were disappointed, but realized that they deserved it—they didn't spend enough time on the work, they didn't study, etc. Also in this category were reasons related to the feedback provided. It adequately explained the reasons for the grade. Twenty-one percent of the reasons given belonged in this category.

Instructor relational issues—This category of reasons related to student perceptions of the instructor. They didn't think the instructor was approachable or they had previous unsuccessful experiences trying to communicate with the instructor. "He had failed at explaining [the material] to me when I had gone to office hours," one wrote. (p. 51) In some cases the students felt the instructor didn't "like" them or was in some way "biased." Reasons here accounted for 22 percent of the responses given for not discussing the disappointing grade.

Judgment of the evaluation—Here students were disappointed but didn't consider the grade all that important. It may have been lower than they expected, but it still wasn't all that bad. Or after having considered the grade, students simply decided they deserved it. In some cases, the grade just wasn't that important to them—it was in a required course or a small part of the overall course grade. Twenty-one percent of the reasons fell into this category.

Student characteristics—These reasons had to do with students just not being comfortable having the conversation. They didn't think they could make the case for a different grade, or they didn't want to try. Some reported feeling embarrassed, others said they were afraid, and some fessed up to being lazy. Sixteen percent of the reasons belonged to this category.

Situational factors—Circumstances prevented some students from discussing the grade. They didn't want to wait to see the professor. They had other priorities, such as exams in other classes. They opted to drop the course. Reasons such as these accounted for 14 percent of the responses.

The reasons for not discussing disappointing grades are a blend of legitimate and not-so-legitimate excuses. Wright offers this wise counsel to teachers: "By giving greater attention to facilitating grade conversations instead of regulating grade disputes, instructors can enhance students' understandings of the diverse benefits of discussing disappointing grades and their legitimate right to initiate them." (p. 57)

REFERENCE

Wright, C.N. (2013). Examining the silence of academic disappointment: A typology of students' reasons for not discussing disappointing grades with instructors. *Journal of the Scholarship of Teaching and Learning, 13* (5), 46-60.

REVIEW AND REFLECTION

WORKSHEET 1

Here's a set of questions that you can use to think more about instructional approaches that develop study skills—those you use and those proposed in this collection of resources. And then there's the question of changes: should you make some? Any potential ideas here that you might implement and assess?

1. What instructional approaches are you using to develop students' study skills? Are you doing enough? Can you find bits and pieces of time to do more?

2. How do you handle reviews in your courses? Who's working harder during those reviews, you or the students? Who stands to benefit the most when they review, you or the students?

3. What about quizzes? What study skills are you using them to develop? Are they developing those skills effectively? If you asked students, what would they see as the role of quizzes in your courses?

4. Do you use in-class review sessions after content chunks on a given topic, before exams? Do any of the activities proposed seem like viable ways to get students involved in reviewing and doing for themselves the hard, messy work of learning?

5. How often do students talk to you when they're disappointed with a grade? How do you encourage those conversations? Do you talk in class or online about actions students might take in response to a disappointing grade? Are there ways you might help students have more realistic grade expectations?

REFLECTION, ACTION, AND RESULTS

WORKSHEET 2

REFLECTION

Resources in the section made me think about these points differently, or, my biggest take away from this section was...

ACTION

❑ I plan to use more in-class review activities, making students use their notes more regularly in class.

❑ I plan to revise my use of quizzes, making sure that my quiz strategies promote good study strategies. I will implement these changes:

1. _____

2. _____

❑ I am going to implement several activities in my in-class review sessions that involve students directly in the review process. Here are the activities I plan to try:

1. _____

2. _____

RESULTS

Here's my plan for assessing the actions I'm planning to take:

After taking those actions, I've seen these differences in my students, their learning and my teaching:

Note Taking
That Promotes Learning

Introduction

When it comes to developing those skills that promote learning, note taking needs to be on the list—first, because it's relevant to college courses and beyond, and second, because so many students aren't very good at it. They'd rather not take notes, preferring to listen or look like they're listening. Some of the reluctance derives from how much easier and safer it seems to just get the teacher's notes or slides. That way there's no quandary about what should be noted, and no worries as to whether it's gotten down correctly. And if class happens to be missed, the teacher's notes provide the necessary backup. Students have been known to make the case for having the teacher's notes strongly and persistently and a lot of teachers provide them. It's easier than resisting and maybe the students will learn more if they have a good set of notes.

The first resource in this section summarizes the research identified reasons why students need to take notes for themselves. A version of those reasons is provided on a handout you can give to students. You can make the case verbally—tell students that they need to take notes but it's more convincing to show students the value of a set of class notes. Section 2: Instructional Strategies that Develop Study Skills includes a set of On-going In-Class Review Activities. It identifies a number of ways to refer to and use student notes in class including challenging students to find things in their notes, answering questions using their notes, reading from their notes, and looking at what other students have in their notes. Behaviors like these demonstrate the value of notes and encourage students to examine their own notes with a more critical eye.

To overcome student resistance to taking notes for themselves and to improve the quality of notes they take, consider giving them skeleton outlines and/or partial notes. There's resource in this section that identifies some characteristics of content that might justify giving students an outline or some notes. There is a bottom line: skeleton outlines and partial notes do not give students all the essential information. They still need to listen and write things down.

Some teachers have gotten creative when it comes to developing note taking practices that accomplish the goals and objectives of their courses. Requiring (or recommending) that students take notes (maybe just sometimes) in specified ways can develop different note taking skills such as summarizing, annotating, outlining or note taking during or after discussions. Do your students ever take notes during or after a discussion? Discussions tend to just end, with no conclusion and nothing in student notes to remind them of what happened and why it might be important. Doing something different with notes every now and then can change how students think about them.

Finally, this section provides resources on the use of laptops and other electronic devices to take notes. Is it a good idea or do students have their electronic devices up and running for reasons not related to note taking? Are their notes different depending on whether they're recorded electronically or longhand? It's a topic being addressed by researchers and the answers are interesting.

Note taking is not a passé learning skill. Some students learn the value notes the hard way—they do poorly on an exam because they didn't have any. Too many students remain unconvinced it's a skill they need to develop. Teachers can change their minds and these resources illustrate some of the ways.

Why Students Need to Take Notes for Themselves

A lot of students don't take notes; others do but don't want to. They'd rather have the teacher make his/her notes and/or slides. Students have been known to ask for them quite persistently. And given the way a lot of students take notes, teachers can be persuaded that giving them a set accurate and organized notes will help them learn. But teacher notes are meaningful to the teacher. They may or may not make sense to the student. And if they do or don't, students, more often than not, simply memorize whatever the teacher makes available. They may "know" the material but understand little of it and retain even less of it. That's not the kind of learning we want for students.

Research across a number of years consistently documents that taking notes benefits students in two ways.

- **Process benefit**—Having to take notes forces students to pay attention, to focus on what's happening. They learn to listen and that's one of those lifetime skills that's not as well developed as it ought to be in most of us.

  But there's another process benefit that occurs when students don't just copy down what the teacher says but put the notes into words meaningful to them. That tightens the connection between what they already know and this new knowledge. And there are strategies you can use to encourage students to get beyond stenography. Let them copy down what you said exactly, then stop and say, "Now you've got 30 seconds to rewrite what I just said in your own words." You can ask several students to read their translations, offer corrections and elaborations, and if merited, praise.

- **Product benefit**—Taking notes provides a record of what was said that can be used for review. Do most students make effective use of the notes they've taken in class? Most do not. I routinely asked my students what they were going to do with their notes; the most common response was, "go over them." "No, no," I used to exclaim. "That's not going to do you any good, you need to get into them!" "Going over" notes basically means rereading them and there's a significant amount of research that questions the effectiveness of rereading as a study strategy. "Rereading has three strikes against it. It is time consuming. It doesn't result in durable memory. And it often involves a kind of unwitting self-deception, as growing familiarity with the text comes to feel like mastery of the material," write educational psychologists Brown, Roediger and McDaniel in their book *Making it Stick: The Science of Successful Learning* (p. 10).

One of the very best things students can do with their notes is to use them to generate questions that can then be used to test knowledge. That's a hard sell to students but there's good research that demonstrates the value of this kind of retrieval practice. The more often you pull something out of memory the easier it becomes to retrieve it.

If you're interested in learning more about the research on note taking, I'd recommend you take a look at the work of Kenneth Kiewra who has devoted most of his career to studying it. His research is first-rate, and he's writes about it accessibly with practical implications clearly spelled out. Here's one of his best pieces.

Kiewra, K. A. (2002). How classroom teachers can help student learn and teach them how to learn. *Theory Into Practice, 41* (2), 71-80.

A Handout for Students on Note Taking

One of the reasons students persistently ask for the teacher's notes or slides is that they aren't sure they're getting down what they should in their notes. So, whatever appears on the slides, they copy down, generally word-for-word. And as they furiously copy what appears on the screen, that pretty much rules out hearing whatever it is the teacher might be saying. Some students, usually those with the better note taking skills, listen for verbal cues. "Here's a definition you should know." "This is an important idea." Here, too, though, they tend to practice stenography, copying down exactly what the teacher says, whether or not they understand it.

So, what about a handout that explains your policy, highlights the reasons why they need to take notes, shares helpful advice, and outlines the ways you plan to help?

My policy on note taking: I don't give students my notes or slides, and here are the reasons why. In this course you'll learn the content better if you take your own notes. My notes make sense to me; you need notes that are meaningful to you. I know this policy isn't particularly popular with students but I plan to support your efforts to take notes. Here's a list of how I will to do that.

1. I will leave my slides up long enough for you to get down what's on them. Consider it a perk for coming to class.

2. I will give you time to write things down. If you need more time, ask for it.

3. I will suggest things that should be in your notes. I will say that directly and clearly. "Here's something I'd recommend you have in your notes." "This is important: Make a note of it."

4. I will encourage you to look for things in your notes. Reviewing notes will be a regular activity in this course.

5. And anytime you have a question about something that's in your notes, be welcome to ask—in class, online or during office hours.

HERE'S A SET OF EVIDENCE-BASED SUGGESTIONS ON TAKING NOTES AND USING THEM TO STUDY:

Do you want to take notes that are helpful when you study? That make it easier to learn the material? And that stand a good chance of improving your exams scores? There's good news. Note-taking has been studied. We know what makes class notes a valuable learning resource.

Take notes using your own words. Yes, every now and then if you want to write down exactly what I say, that's okay. But in general use words that make sense to you. If you are copying down exactly what I say, put it in quotes and then when you review those notes, take what's in those quotations and rewrite them in your own words.

Write more than you think you need to. When you hear something in class, it makes sense, but you'll be hearing about lots of content in the weeks between exams. So even though three words are all you think you'll need to remember it, you'll be glad that you added more details when you study those notes later on.

Review your notes the same day you've taken them. A drag. . .and you don't have time, but you don't have to spend a lot of time on this first review. Think five minutes. The point of this review is to make sure that what you've got in your notes makes sense. This is also the time to add more details or to indicated you might need to add more details from the reading. What we talked about in class should still be fresh in your mind.

Review your notes regularly. You can get away with cramming in some classes, I know that. If you talk with students who've taken this course, I'm guessing they'll tell you it doesn't work well for my exams. What the research says and what I'm convinced works better is ongoing regular review and here as well, we're not talking about endless hours of study. When you sit down to do the reading, start by opening your notes. Pick a day (not just the previous day) and go through those notes. When I ask a question that you can't answer, see if you can find the answer in your notes.

Decide how you're going to take notes—electronically or by hand. Here's what the research is uncovering. Electronically, you get more material in your notes. A good thing? Well, not entirely. More notes is better but with a keyboard there's a tendency to transcribe, to key in what you hear. Students taking notes electronically put less of the content in their own words. Because writing is slower, it forces you to make decisions about what to write and means you are more likely to be using your own words. And then there's the distraction danger. I try to be fascinating to listen to, but sometimes I'm not, and with the wonderful world of the internet just a click away…

Share notes with a study buddy. Don't give them away to somebody who has nothing to give you in return, but trade notes with somebody else who's working to take good notes. Do they have something important that you've missed? Have they described something in a way that makes it easier to understand? Talk to each other about what's in your notes.

Evaluate your notes. Figure out whether they're helping you learn the material and get the grade you need in the course. Look hard at the questions you missed on the exam. Did you have the information in your notes you needed to answer those questions? Are you missing important information? Not writing enough? Not writing notes that make sense to you after the fact?

Skeleton Outlines and Partial Notes

Consider a middle ground between giving students your notes/slides and expecting them to take notes for themselves. Provide skeleton outlines or partial notes with plenty of room for students to fill in the details. In some circumstances it makes sense to do so. Here are the situations in which some notes from the teacher can expedite student note taking and learning.

- **The material is complex containing lots of new ideas and information.** A set of notes that lists the most important points, the central concepts can prevent information overload. These teacher notes might include key terms, brief definitions, or short statements describing new concepts. Beneath, there's room and encouragement for students to write in an example, a question, or salient elaboration offered in the teacher's discussion of the topic.

- **The organization hard to follow.** If the ideas are hard to connect or the relationships between primary and secondary points isn't obvious, particularly to a novice, a skeleton outline that lists the main and their supporting points can keep students from feeling lost and confused. They can focus on understanding the ideas rather than trying to figure out how the material fits together. Again, it's a skeleton outline with space provided for students to fill in the details.

- **There's lots of new and unfamiliar terminology.** An outline with a header something like, "By the end of the session, you'll want to have definitions and examples for each of these terms" encourages students to listen for the key terms. Listing them also ensures that they are spelled correctly. Using concise definitions helps note taking as does including at least some terms familiar to the student. If the definition needs to include complex terminology, you could provide those definitions. Students can be given time to try to put the definition into words that make sense to them, or they can be encouraged to add examples.

- **Provide any graphs, tables, diagrams, figures, models, or other graphic representations that students need to have in their notes.** There is some research indicating that visual materials end up being the least accurate of all the content in student notes. In general, it's a good idea to provide the shape of the structure with students then responsible for adding the data, labels, or other written components of the visual material.

To persuade students of the value of skeleton outlines and notes that still require completion, you might want to tell them about a 2008 study where one cohort of students got complete sets of the teacher's notes and another cohort got partial/skeleton notes. Students who got the partial notes to which they then added material got statistically significant better scores on the third and fourth exams, they did better on conceptual questions on the final, and they got higher course grades.

REFERENCE

Cornelius, T. L., and Owen-DeSchryver, J., (2008). Differential effects of full and partial notes on learning outcomes and attendance. *Teaching of Psychology, 35* (1), 6-12.

Two Unique Strategies that Improved Note Taking

Students in a social psychology research methods course completed this three part note-restructuring assignment: they had to submit a typed copy of their restructured and reorganized class notes; they had to prepared a 30 word or less summary of the lecture, called the "foot" (after the rabbi who was asked by a skeptic to summarize all of Judaism while standing on one foot); and they selected one detail which they described in 150 words, called the "sock" (after John Wooden, the famous UCLA basketball coach whose players practiced putting on their socks during the first squad meeting, because blisters can cost games and seemingly trivial details can be crucial). Students were randomly assigned to complete this assignment. The hypothesis that they would score higher on test questions when they did this restructuring was confirmed pretty dramatically. The gain was equivalent to 1.1 standard deviation or a full grade.

REFERENCE

Cohen, D., Kim, E., Tan, J., and Windelmes, M., (2013). A note-restructuring intervention increases students' exam scores. *College Teaching, 61* (3), 95-99.

Economics professor Mark Maier assigns a "rotating note taker" in his courses. This student serves as the class note taker, posting his or her notes on the course learning management system before the next class session. The note takers' notes are graded pass/fail and count for one percent of the final course grade. If it's a fail, the student learns why and is assigned another day to take and post class notes.

Having a designated student taking and posting notes does not relieve individual students of the responsibility to take their own notes. "The posted notes serve as an alternative to the student's own notes…" (p.146) They may clarify a concept, emphasize a different part of it, add more detail or offer a different perspective.

Maier introduces the assignment on day one. He recruits a student familiar with the course learning management system to provide the first set of class notes. He also puts instructions about posting notes on the learning management system, offers recommendations about attaching files, and suggests making references to the text instead of trying to reproduce complicated graphs. If the class is large, Maier has two students taking and posting notes for each class session.

Here's a list of benefits that accrue from the strategy:
- Students report that they find the posted notes helpful when they are reviewing for tests. It's an opportunity to check what they have written down with what someone else has in their notes.

- If a student knows that everyone in the class is going to look at his or her notes and that the teacher is going to evaluate them, that motivates careful note-taking. The note taker and the rest of the class benefit by getting a set of notes taken by someone focused on the task.

- Students who aren't good note takers have the chance to see what a good set of notes looks like. Maier reports that improves the quality of the notes weaker students start posting.

- If a student misses class, they have access to a set of notes.

- The strategy demonstrates the teacher's commitment to student note-taking. It's more persuasive than telling students that taking notes is a good thing.

REFERENCE

Maier, M. H., (2016). Rotating note taker. *College Teaching, 64* (3), 148.

Discussions and Notes

Discussions are often transient instructional events. They start, proceed and then end, but often without much or any lingering impact. Because students tend to think the only comments worth noting come from the teacher, they rarely (maybe never) write down anything a peer might say. And teachers seldom take time to summarize discussions. If asked a few days later about the discussion, most students are hard pressed to remember anything.

Notes taken before or during a discussion can help to focus the exchange and lead it to more interesting places. And notes jotted down after a discussion provide a record that can trigger memories of the event. They also make it easier for teachers to link new content to previous discussions.

Teachers rarely address discussion note taking—why it might be valuable and how to do it. Here are some ways to give notes a role in framing, directing, and preserving a class discussion. Discussion note taking is another opportunity to develop note-taking skills and to reinforce their importance.

- **Bring notes to the discussion.** Specify the discussion topic beforehand and have each student come to the discussion with a written question or comment. Pass out index cards and have students write their question or comments on one side of the card and their name on the other. (This can happen electronically, if you prefer.) Collect the cards, leaf through them, and use good questions and comments throughout the discussion. Any student who's submitted a question or comment gets a participation point. Any student whose question or comment is used get two points.

- **Stop for reflection.** Stop the discussion and have students to write something down: a comment that made them think, a description that helped them understand, a question they have about something somebody said, or where they think the discussion needs to head next. The writing prompt can be even more generic: "Stop. You've got 30 seconds to write down whatever you're thinking about on this discussion topic." Gary Hafer in his book *Embracing Writing: Ways to Teach Reluctant Writers in Any Course* recommends that during these stops for reflection, teachers participate by writing down their thoughts. Have some students read what they've written. Is it a comment or question that merits further discussion?

- **Ask some students to be the discussion note takers.** If two or three volunteer, no problem. You can post their notes on the LMS or distribute them some other way. And consider this participation. It gives introverts a way to comfortably contribute and provides students with a record of the discussion.

- **Make time to summarize the discussion and let students do the summarizing.** "You've got two or three minutes. Make some notes about the discussion. What's worth remembering?

What do you want to think about more? What might make a good short answer essay question?" Then have students share summaries with each other and finish with several read to the whole class.

- **Keep referring to the discussion.** Use it! "Remember that discussion we had about civil disobedience? Look at your notes. Do you have anything there that relates to what we're talking about now?" Or, "Take a look at Jayna's discussion notes on the course website and review the comments there about when civil disobedience breaks the law. Would that be justified in this case?" And then there's the possibility of using something in those discussion notes as the frame for a short essay question on the next quiz.

Laptop Zones

Laptops and tablet devices of various sorts are everywhere in college classrooms at this point. Students use them to take notes. Keying is quicker than writing notes longhand, and typed notes are subsequently easier to read. Faculty have two legitimate worries; students are using their devices for activities other than note-taking, and bright screens filled with colorful graphics can distract more than just the student who's not taking notes. The authors referenced below think this is an especially serious problem in large lecture halls where students sit close together and it's all but impossible for the teacher to control who's doing what with their electronic devices.

They wondered whether laptop zones might be a solution. To test their theory, they designated laptop zones in two sections of a large, introductory biology course. Two other sections where students sat without seating restrictions acted as the control.

The authors' analysis is well-designed and creative. It's explained in detail in this research article. Here's a rundown of their findings. If they are of interest, this is an excellent article that extensively references related research.

- There was no difference in attendance rates between the unrestricted seating sections and those with laptop zones; nor was there any difference in the number of students who used laptops to take notes.

- The percentage of laptop users who were off-task (that is, who had non-course content on their screens, as observed from the back of the room) was significantly higher in the zoned than in the control sections. Forty percent of the students off-task were using social media, including Facebook, instant messaging, and video chat.

- The average percentage of laptops that were off-task at any given time during the lecture was 17 percent in the control sections. This observational-based percentage is lower that student self-reported percentages, as documented by other research.

- Free-response survey questions gave students the opportunity to indicate why they selected to take notes by hand or on the computer. The most frequent response among those taking notes by hand was that the process "facilitates learning." Those using laptops most frequently reported that it was "convenient."

- As for performance: "Academic performance, based on exam points earned, was not significantly different for paper users in zoned and control sections, indicating laptop use did not impair the overall achievement of surrounding students. However, there was a correlation between exam performance and note taking preference: paper note takers scored significantly higher and laptop users scored significantly lower than predicted by pre-class academic indicators" (p. 1300).

- Students in all sections were opposed to banning laptops. Only 10 percent supported that policy. When asked about restricting laptop use to designated zones, 50 percent of the note takers in the control sections supported that policy; 82 percent of those in the zoned classes did. "After exposure to zoning the preference of both paper and laptop users shifts significantly in favor of zoning" (p. 1305).

Here's the research team's overall conclusion: "Although the creation of a laptop-free zone did not affect overall student performance, zoning had a positive impact on the class environment and student attitudes. Although zoned laptop users engaged in more off-task behavior, that wasn't associated with a decrease in performance." They offer an important caveat: "Because the variable we manipulated in this study was zoning, not laptop use, the underlying causes for why laptop users underperformed are not known" (p. 1307).

REFERENCE

Aguilar-Roca, N.M., Williams, A.E., and O'Dowd, D.K., (2012). The impact of laptop-free zones on student performance and attitudes in large lectures. *Computers & Education, 59,* 1300–1308.

Laptops or Longhand?

There are lots of reasons and research that support students taking their own notes as opposed to re- lying on teacher-provided notes and/or slides—another resource in this section highlights the rea- sons and the research. What's changed now is how students are taking notes. Some 2012 research (cited in the reference below) reported that almost a third of student were using laptops to take notes. With the diversity of electronic devices currently available that percentage may now be larger. Of interest to researchers now is the question of whether it makes a difference if students take notes electronically or write them longhand. Four studies (all published since 2012) have considered that question and all four agree on a couple of points.

- **Students taking notes electronically record more information.** That would seem to be a good thing—the more complete the notes, the better. But there's a problem with what ends up in electronically taken notes. There's more copied down material, word-for-word what the teacher said. It's a stenographic form of note taking what the researchers describe as a non-generative transcription process.

- **Students who take notes longhand have more of the lecture ideas in their own words.** They have fewer words, which is understandable. Most of us can key in words faster than we can write them. Students taking longhand notes use more generative processes. They make more decisions about what to write and do more to make that content understandable to them.

In terms of achievement, findings from the four studies are inconsistent. In one study, if the notes were not reviewed, those taking notes on a laptop had higher achievement scores. A second study found the opposite. If notes were reviewed, the results were again mixed. Part of the inconsistency may be the result of the different study designs.

The most recent study (referenced below) does an excellent job of highlighting the previous research and incorporating aspects of those studies in their design. They systematically investigated the process and product function of note taking as well as the medium (laptop or longhand) in terms of achieve- ment. The process function relates to the benefits accrued by writing something down rather than just hearing it. The product function involves the value that comes from having a set of notes after the fact (as in when you need to review for the exam). This research team examined these variables using more authentic course material and for the first time looked at how visual material was recorded and whether recording images affected image-related achievement.

Here's a sum of their findings:

- Laptop note takers accrued more process benefits of note taking. Copying down exactly what they were hearing required minimal cognitive processing and so at that moment they were learning more. They had notes that were more complete.

- Longhand note takers gain more product benefits. When they looked at their notes, they had content that made sense to them because they used more of their own words. They also had more visual materials in their notes.

- "When there was ample processing time during review, the more generative longhand notes proved to be a better review source than the more transcription-oriented laptop notes." (p. 963) Said a bit more clearly and directly, if students aren't going to review their notes, whether they take them electronically or by hand probably doesn't make much difference. But if students are going to review their notes, those taken longhand provide a better review than those taken electronically.

As these researchers note, this research is in its infancy and these studies are still not replicating actual note taking conditions. For example, in order to control for extraneous variables, students in these studies are not reviewing their notes two or three weeks after they've taken them or reviewing notes taken in six or seven different class sessions. They are taking one set of notes, and either not reviewing them and answering test questions about the lecture or reviewing those notes shortly and briefly after they've taken them and answering test questions about the lecture.

At this point, the findings are definitive in terms of what ends up in laptop and longhand notes, but less conclusive as to the effects of the medium on achievement. However, if students plan to review their notes (and we would hope that most students do plan to review), the better bet is to go with longhand notes.

REFERENCE

Luo, L., Kiewra, K. A., Flanigan, A. E. and Peteranetz, M. (2018). Laptop versus longhand note taking: effects on lecture notes and achievement. *Instructional Science, 46,* 947-971.

REVIEW AND REFLECTION

WORKSHEET 1

Here's a set of questions that you can use to think more about how students do or don't take notes in your class. This section highlighted some instructional practices that develop good note taking skills. That leads to the change questions raised on the next worksheet. Could you be doing a better job of developing students' note taking skills? If so, how?

1. Are your students taking notes or using yours? Why do they pressure you for yours? Are there ways you could help them make sure they have what they need in their notes?

2. Do you encourage students to find things their notes when you ask questions or remind them of something they should know? Should you do this more? Any of the ways proposed in the resources seem like options that might work in your courses?

3. Say you told students they'd be having a quiz on the material you're presenting today, and they'll be able to use their notes during the quiz. Do you think that would change how they took notes? Do you think they might see the difference?

4. How many of your students are taking notes with electronic devices? Have you ever looked at any of those notes? It might be interesting to get a set of notes taken electronically and another written longhand from the same class session. Are there differences? Are those differences worth discussing online or in class?

5. Have you ever given students skeleton outlines or partial notes? What would you see as assets and liabilities of doing so?

REFLECTION, ACTION, AND RESULTS

WORKSHEET 2

REFLECTION

Resources in the section made me think about these points differently, or, my biggest take away from this section was...

ACTION

❏ I plan to have a discussion with my students about the value of note taking as a skill. I will ask them to suggest things I can do that would help them take better notes.

❏ I plan to occasionally provide students with skeleton outline or partial notes to see if that strategy improves the quality of their notes.

❏ I'm going to ask several students who are taking notes electronically if I can take a look at their notes. I'd like to see if they are copying down lots of content verbatim.

❏ I am going to implement a couple of innovative note-taking strategies. Here're the activities I plan to try:

1. _____

2. _____

RESULTS

Here's my plan for assessing the actions I'm planning to take:

After taking those actions, I've seen these differences in my students, their learning and my teaching:

Reading
Skills

Introduction

Many students do not arrive in our courses with college-level reading skills. That usually ends up meaning a couple of things. First off, they don't like to read and will disregard teacher announcements and syllabus admonitions telling them that reading is a required part of the course. They'll come to class, sit quietly, take a few notes and see what happens if they're in class and haven't done the reading. If nothing happens, then maybe they don't have to or can put it off until just before the exam. A depressing number of students are coming to class not having done the reading, according to research cited in the resource, Doing the Reading and Developing College Level Reading Skills.

Students especially don't like reading "boring" textbooks. To them, what's in the reading is complicated, unfamiliar and doesn't seem all that relevant. What's most important? What do they need to know? How does what's in the text relate to what's happening in class? Bottom line: for many students, the ideal courses wouldn't have textbooks or required readings.

Without good skills, students often resort to dubious approaches when they do read. With fluorescent markers, they underline whole paragraphs, if not whole pages. Check out the resource in this section that highlights differences between what faculty and students underline. When students do read course materials, they're regularly interrupted by a range of distractions; TV, music, and electronic devices of various sorts. They skip over the words they don't know. They don't stop and reread what's confusing. The idea of interacting with the text—thinking about the contents, relating the it what's been talked about in class, working to understand a passage, keeping mental track of what they've read in light of what they're reading now—all of these close reading strategies necessary to understanding text material are used as the exception rather than the rule.

Complicating these deficient reading skills are college courses in every discipline packed with content. What teachers often miss is that reading skills can be developed as students do their course assigned readings. The Assignments and Activities section of the Doing the Reading and Developing College Level Reading Skills resource proposes various approaches that get students doing the reading and at the same time direct the student to read in ways that develop reading skills. They're great examples of how content can be married with process.

The most common solution to getting students doing the reading is the regularly scheduled or surprise reading quiz. Research verifies that quizzes do get students coming to class and keeping up with the reading. Unfortunately, though, quizzes can also reinforce poor reading habits. If the quiz questions are simple, straightforward queries designed solely to see who's done the reading, students can quickly become quiz-wise. Then they read the material in search of answers and that approach doesn't do much to develop good reading skills. But there are ways to use quizzes that do get students reading in more productive ways. Some of those approaches are described in this section and other can be found in Section 2: Instructional Approaches that Develop Study Skills.

Another liability with quizzes is how they get students doing the reading because they have to, not because they want to. It's troubling to think of students graduating without realizing that a lifetime of professional reading awaits a majority of them. They will be expected to learn on their own by reading and most of those materials won't be easy. Is there any way teachers can model the value of reading? There's a resource that offers an answer to that question.

It's probably not realistic to expect college students to fall in love with reading our course materials—although occasionally a few do. It is realistic to attempt to use assigned readings in ways that develop those skills and to disavow students of some of their bad reading habits.

Doing the Reading and Developing College-Level Reading Skills

Information, Ideas, and Resources

Relevant Research Findings—The study below cites multiple studies, starting in the 1970's, documenting that on any given day only 20–30 percent of the students have completed the assigned reading.

Researchers asked a 423 cross-disciplinary student cohort how likely they were to complete assigned readings if the teacher used announced reading quizzes, mandatory reading guides/questions, short required writing assignments, required journaling, randomly called on students to answer questions, unannounced reading quizzes, or optional reading guides. Students rated announced quizzes, mandatory reading questions, and short required writing assignments as the approaches most likely to get them doing the reading.

Hatteberg, S. J. and Steffy, K., (2013). Increasing reading compliance of undergraduates: An evaluation of compliance methods. *Teaching Sociology, 41* (4), 346-352.

Quiz Options that Promote Better Reading

Two-question, online quiz, due before class— "In the process of collecting assessment data in my introductory course, I made a startling and disappointing discovery. For the most part, students simply were not bothering to read. . .the introductory survey textbook that I assigned." (p. 385) Howard's solution was a two-question online quiz, due two hours before class. The first question was multiple-choice that forced students to consider evidence presented in the reading. He favored questions on text material that challenged conventional thinking. The second short-answer question required students to summarize or synthesize information in text. Howard graded the quizzes before class and used some of the responses (both strong and weak ones) to launch class discussion of the topic.

Howard. J. R., (2004). Just in time teaching in sociology or how I convinced my students to actually read the assignment. *Teaching Sociology, 32*, 385-90.

Take the quiz with notes—Students take detailed notes on the reading because they're allowed to use those notes during the quiz. The pay-off is a good (or better) set of notes for use during exam preparation. Resaei reports that open-note quizzing coupled with collaboration resulted in significantly higher final exam scores in his quantitative research methods course. If you want to improve the notes students take in class, this approach may accomplish that objective just as well.

Rezaei, A. R., (2015). Frequent collaborative quiz taking and conceptual learning. *Active Learning in Higher Education, 16* (3), 187-196.

Group quizzing—Group quizzing approaches with questions on assigned readings get students doing the reading primarily because of peer pressure. The vast majority of students don't want to look unprepared or foolish in front of their peers. They develop reading skills because students must recall and explain what they read. Find some group quizzing structures in the Creative Quiz Options in Instructional Strategies that Develop Study Skills (p. 43).

Assignments and Activities the Promote Reading and Develop Skills

Paraphrase text content—Lloyd assigns various kinds of required written work (worksheets, short papers and online discussions) in which students respond to materials in the primary and secondary texts used in his theology courses. Students must follow this rule: no quotations from the reading, only their paraphrases of the ideas. And, for every sentence they write that uses information in the text, they must provide a page number citation. If back-to-back sentences use text content, that's fine, but they must include the page number.
Lloyd, D., (2016). No quotations, always citations. *Teaching Theology and Religion, 19* (4), 387.

Reading logs—Students completed a reflective reading log assignment with 10 entries. Each entry responded to one of the essays assigned for the week. Manarin shared information on nine different reading strategies. The students had to select one of those strategies and use it when they read the essay. In the entry they had to comment on how well that strategy worked with the essay's content. Students had 15 minutes in class to write their entries and this assignment counted for 10 percent of their grade with only modest teacher feedback provided. One student wrote of the assignment, "Doing these logs over the course of the semester has really given me insight into how I read." (p. 292)
Manarin, K., (2012). Reading value: Student choice in reading strategies." *Pedagogy, 12* (2), 281-297.

Student generated reading questions—Students in an upper-division biochemistry course generated questions from assigned readings, one question for each of 11 readings. The assignment stipulated that the questions could not be factual but must describe conceptual problems. "In generating their own questions, students reveal how they think about a topic, as well as the way in which they make connections between topics as they extend upon and construct new knowledge." (p. 31)
Offerdahl, E. G., and Montplaisir, L, (2014). Student-generated reading questions: Diagnosing student thinking with diverse formative assessments." *Biochemistry and Molecular Biology Education, 42* (1), 29-38.

Reading Groups—Students were assigned to reading groups which meet regularly. Each student rotated through a set of roles: discussion leader, passage master, devil's advocate, creative connector, and recorder. They came to group meetings having done the reading and with prepared materials reflective of their role. The group then discussed the readings for a designated amount of time. This article offers excellent advice on implementing reading groups in a course.
Parrott, H. M. and Cherry, E., (2011). Using structured reading groups to facilitate deep learning." *Teaching Sociology, 39* (4), 354-370.

Reading Responses—These authors make a strong case against quizzes, proposing instead that students complete written reading responses for each of 29 reading assignments in the course. Students may choose any of the following responses for any of the readings: 1) connect to the text as in interact with it (underline, write comments, questions), then generate five questions and answer two of them; 2) summarize the readings and visualize key ideas with graphic organizers or charts; 3) prepare a reading response journal which lists questions or comments after each section of the reading; 4) study with one or two classmates with one person preparing a written report of what the group discussed; or 5) create a song or rap which is recorded and submitted.

Roberts, J. C., and Roberts, K. A., (2008). Deep reading, cost/benefit, and the construction of meaning: Enhancing reading comprehension and deep learning in sociology courses. *Teaching Sociology, 36*, 125-140.

Reading Prompts—Tomasek believes that prompts and questions can be "used to orient students with a critical reading stance and to guide their thinking as they read." (p. 128) His overarching goal is to help student "synthesize and respond to the big ideas from the reading selection as opposed to mining facts or details." (p. 128) He organizes the prompts around six categories; 1) identification of problem or issue, 2) making connections, 3) interpretation of evidence, 4) challenging assumptions, 5) making applications, and 6) taking a different point of view. He writes the prompts in first person so that they "promote active and personal learning." (p. 128) For example, "How is what I'm reading different from what I already know? Why might this difference exist?"

Tomasek, T., (2009). Critical reading: Using reading prompts to promote active engagement with text." *International Journal of Teaching and Learning in Higher Education*, 2009, 21 (1), 127-132.

Course Preparation Assignment—The success of discussion-based courses depends on students coming to the discussion having thoughtfully done the reading. This assignment prepares students for discussion. Posted online (one for almost every class session) each course preparation assignment follows the same format: introduces the topic, states the objective, offers a bit of background information, and then provides the question or prompt that students answer. Students bring these written assignments with them to class. Sometimes they are used in small group discussions that precede the whole class discussion. They are graded on a credit/no credit bases.

Yamane, D., (2006). Course preparation assignments: A strategy for creating discussion-based courses. *Teaching Sociology, 34* (July), 236-248.

Making the Most of Highlighting

A lot of students are in love with their highlighters, especially those bright, fluorescent-colored ones. They use them to highlight course materials, sometimes underlining whole pages of text. When I first saw a text so fluorescent that it all but glowed, I wondered why in the world somebody would spend that much time underlining. Later I understood it was really a cry for help. "I can't tell what's important, so I'll just highlight the entire section so I don't miss something." Highlighting can be a useful way of interacting with text, but it needs to be done in a thoughtful way.

A creatively designed study analyzed what faculty, seniors, and first-year students underlined in a piece of primary research in biology. The study contained content familiar to the faculty members. The seniors were biology majors taking a capstone course, and the freshmen were first-year biology students. The questions that motivated the study were pretty straightforward: How do students identify what's important in an article like this? Assuming they don't tackle the task the same way experts do, what do they do differently, and how can they be taught to read more like the experts?

The results weren't all that unexpected. Faculty readers pretty much agreed on what was and wasn't important in the article. The seniors and the freshmen didn't agree all that much with each other or with the faculty, although the seniors agreed more closely with the faculty than the freshmen did. The researchers concluded that the seniors had developed some degree of scientific literacy during their undergraduate careers. (If more specific details are of interest, find them in the study.)

It's the study design that I found most intriguing, and I wondered if it might be a strategy that could help students interact with their assigned readings more effectively. Start by assigning students some course-related material to read and highlight—you can decide if they need a few points to take the task seriously. Then give them a copy of the material with your highlights and encourage discussion on how the two compare and contrast. You could also challenge students to consider how they decide what needs to be underlined. Are there ways to tell when something is important in a text, an essay, or a short story? Is highlighting useful only in identifying what's important? What about underlining things you don't understand or passages that relate to content being talked about in class or covered in previous chapters?

The study authors point out that novice science readers usually approach text in a linear fashion. They start at the beginning and read through to the end. I'd say that's pretty typical of how most students approach all kinds of text. In the case of science studies, the authors note that experienced readers tend to start with the title and the abstract, using those to decide if a paper is of interest. If it is, they often jump to results and consider the findings. Then they might look at the methodology to ascertain if it's sound, and finally, depending on their level of interest, they consider the review of literature and discussion sessions. I suspect the way experts read content in every field is somewhat unique. The question is when and how are these approaches taught to students?

Some observations get pointed out pretty regularly in this blog—sorry for repeating this one. Most of our students don't have college-level reading skills. One of the reasons they don't do their reading is because it's hard, and just like the rest of us, they find excuses to avoid doing what's difficult. This is why it is essential that we do what we can to promote the development of skills that make reading college-level materials a less daunting task. A more strategic approach to highlighting is an easy place to help students explore how they know when something's important and whether that's the only reason to highlight. From there we might venture into what they can do with what they've underlined when they're studying for an exam.

REFERENCE

Gallo, M. and Rinaldo, V., (2012). Towards a mastery understanding of critical reading in biology: The use of highlighting by students to assess their value judgment of the importance of primary literature. *Journal of Microbiology & Biology Education, 13* (2), 142-149.

Actions that Underscore of Importance Assigned Readings

Sometimes a bit of drama can be convincing. How you ever considered doing some show and tell with the textbook? I'm referring to actions that show how much you value and rely on the readings you've selected and assigned. You don't say they're important—that's a tired old message—you show it.

- Regularly bring text or reading selections to class. Hold them, wave them around, open them up, look things up. Let students see you using them (if not with joy and wonder, at least with purpose and with pleasure).

- Expect students to bring their books or reading materials to class. As students are settling in and unpacking, offer this reminder: "Be sure you get out your text. We're going to be using it in class today." As you wander around the room before class give a "good job" or "high fives" to any student who has his or her book out on the desk.

- During class read something from the text or ask a student to read a key sentence or paragraph. Can you be shameless? "If I were prepping for an exam in this class, that's something I'd want underlined in my text."

- Ask a question and tell everyone to find the answer in the book. Then have a student read the answer from the book. Don't cave in on this. Students are used to getting answers from the teacher. There's work involved in having to look it up. If lots of students are waiting around for a student to cares to look it up, okay the first time. But next time change the rules: "you've got two minutes, look up the answer. I'm going to randomly call on someone to read us the answer."

- Underline something important in the text and show it to students. "Look here on p. 48, I've underlined a key insight? Did you underline that in your book? You might want to." Teachers who tried this (and the suggestion above) report that next time in class they're seeing a lot more books and highlighters.

- If a student asks a question that's ably answered in the text, don't answer the question but refer the student to the text. Make that a specific reference. "You know what? On page 57 there's an excellent answer to your question. Check it out and if you have a follow-question or comment, I'm happy to talk more about what you're asking."

- Refer to graphic illustrations in the text. "Everyone turn to page 85 and check out Table 2a. Take a look at it and then tell me what you see that relates to X." Don't put the table on a slide. It's about letting there be consequences, if you aren't bringing your book to class. You can't see the table, or you have to look around and see if someone will share. And who's responsible for not being able to see the table you are talking about? Hasn't the teacher announced several times that having books in class is important?

- Start class by asking one or two students to read something they've underlined in the assigned reading. The follow-up question asks why they deemed that important enough to underline. It's a quick and easy way to raise the issue of how a student knows what to underline.

Finally, an approach used by a sociology colleague of mine that values the text in an unusual way: He changed texts in his intro course every five years. The year before the change, he had student groups in several sections review potential texts—each group reviewed one text. The assignment was elaborate; students had to do things with the text (including read a lot of it), they had to identify its features and survey classmates as to their preferences. In the end they prepared a written review and then rated the book across a number of criteria. The book with the highest scores he used for the next five years. In the syllabus and regularly in subsequent courses, he pointed out that the text was student selected. Yes, he reviewed all the potential texts first. The groups only reviewed books he deemed appropriate for the course. He had evidence that having a student-selected text changed how students felt about the book. He consistently had the highest student ratings in his department on the end-of-course rating question about the quality of the text. They valued it more; one hopes that meant they read it more.

REVIEW AND REFLECTION

WORKSHEET 1

Here's another round of questions that aim to encourage you to consider your students' reading skills. Teachers who assign reading tend to love reading and that makes it hard to relate to students who don't. But reading skills are essential on many personal and professional fronts. So how do we develop those skills and an appreciation for them? Could you be doing more? Any ideas here that might be something you could implement?

1. What do you know about when and how students are doing the reading in your courses? Are you relying on your impressions or have you actually asked, collected information in a more or less systematic way? What kind of grade can a student in your course get without doing the reading? Is your answer to that question based on evidence?

2. Have you taken a look at some student texts and seen how much they're highlighting? Are they highlighting too much? Have you talked with them about how they decide what to underline? Are there any other ways that might be interacting with the text?

3. If you're using quizzes to keep students up with the reading, what features of those quizzes actually focus on and develop their reading skills?

4. What happens to students in your course who show up not having done the reading? No, I'm not suggesting public humiliation, but if it's okay to be in class unprepared, then what does that say about the importance of reading in the course?

5. What's the relationship between content in the text and content covered in class? How would students describe that relationship if you asked them? Are students seeing the connections between the readings and the activities and assignments of the course?

REFLECTION, ACTION, AND RESULTS

WORKSHEET 2

REFLECTION

Resources in the section made me think about these points differently, or, my biggest take away from this section was...

ACTION

❑ I will survey my students and find out when they do the reading, how long it takes them to read an assignment, and what they see as the relationship between the assigned readings and the content covered in course sessions.

❑ I will try in my teaching to regularly underscore the value of the material I've assigned students to read. Specifically, I will do that by:

1. _____

2. _____

3. _____

❑ I will re-examine how I use reading quizzes and incorporate at least one activity that focuses on reading skill development.

RESULTS

Here's my plan for assessing the actions I'm planning to take:

After taking those actions, I've seen these differences in my students, their learning and my teaching:

Study GROUPS

Introduction

Some students prefer to study alone; some like to study with others. Beyond personal preference stands the best way to learn content and skills of the course. Some content and most skills can only be learned alone; other material is more easily mastered with others. Most content is learned better if the collaboration takes place after individual study. Students who haven't done the reading aren't going to contribute much useful to any discussion of it.

Learning with others, in this case via a study group, is helpful on a number of different fronts. Study groups are safer places to ask questions and to admit confusion or failure. Sometimes a student explanation can make more sense than the teacher's. Students use language familiar to other students. Having just recently understood something, they can identify barriers and what caused a breakthough. Figuring things out with others builds confidence, especially for students who aren't empowered learners.

All sorts of research documents that students can learn from each other. Other research, plus all sorts of firsthand experience provides evidence that learning in groups doesn't happen automatically. It didn't in three sections of a large introductory biology course where the exam scores of students in study groups were not higher than students who studied alone. Interestingly though, 85 percent of those in the groups believed being in a study group helped their grade on the first exam. A bit more than half the 700 students in this cohort reported that they never participated in study groups. (Rybczynski, S. M. and Schussler, E. E. (2011) Student use of out-of-class study groups in an introductory undergraduate biology course. *Cell Biology Education—Life Sciences Education, 10* (Spring), 74-82.) There's more recent research on study groups summarized in this section and the conclusions reported there are more positive.

Most of the resources in this section propose ways to encourage student participation in study groups and improve the quality of their experiences in them. The resources also assume that teachers with heavy loads, large courses and/or research responsibilities do not have time to set up, organize, and manage student study groups. But teachers can encourage students to form and participate in study groups—there's a resource that identifies a number of ways they can do so. Also included in the section is one teacher's model for student-run study groups. There's a handout for students that proposes the reasons why they ought to consider studying with others and offers advice on making those study sessions productive.

If study groups "register" with the teacher, their exam scores can be averaged. If that average happens to be higher than the class average that may motivate more participation in study groups. As teachers and scholars, most of us know firsthand how much we can learn from and with others. We should be encouraging student participation in study groups and providing the support that helps them work in those groups productively.

Study Groups: A Research Analysis

Maybe we should be making a stronger pitch for student-led study groups. There are all sorts of research documenting how students can learn from each other. But, as regularly noted here and elsewhere, that learning doesn't happen automatically, and some of us worry that it's not likely to occur in a study group where there's no supervision and distractions abound. Recent findings should encourage us to give study groups a second look.

The groups in this research involved two or more students working together outside class in groups they formed and facilitated. A cohort of 463 undergraduates enrolled at 38 different institutions and majoring in five different fields answered questions about their study group experiences—if they studied with others, why they chose to do so, what they did in those groups, and how helpful they found the experience.

A large majority of this cohort (78 percent) reported that they participated in at least one group study session per semester with a median of four sessions. This percentage is a bit higher than has been reported in previous research. Students said they opted to study with others because the professor encouraged it and their peers invited them. Their groups handled all the meeting logistics and members decided collectively what they would do during the session.

And here's what's impressive: the top three study strategies students reported using in these groups were asking each other questions, discussing course materials, and quizzing each other. Those are evidence-based strategies. Asking questions and discussing the content are elaborative activities that deepen learning, and test-enhanced learning (testing with questions) enhances memory by providing retrieval practice. "Each of these has substantial empirical support with regard to benefits for long-term retention, falling into the category of 'desirable difficulties.' [a la Bjork]." (p. 18)

And there's more good news. The data showed that a student's GPA correlated positively with how frequently evidence-based study strategies were used—particularly, reflective elaboration of the content (mnemonics), generation (making outlines, flashcards, study guides), and spacing (shorter group meetings but more of them). Now, with correlational research, it's not possible to say whether these learning skills are being developed in study groups or whether students who already use these approaches tend to gravitate toward studying with others.

Students said they chose to study with others in hopes it would improve their understanding of the material. And most of them reported that it did. More than 60 percent said their level of learning in study groups was somewhat more or a lot more than they learned when studying individually. Almost 70 percent said that being in a study group increased their motivation to study. Interesting, however, only about 20 percent said they preferred studying in a group compared with almost 50 percent who said they always or mostly preferred to study alone. Could this preference reflect the many bad group experiences students have had?

Findings like these give us reasons to encourage students to study together, and we can use these results to offer advice with the potential to improve what happens in those groups.

Keep the group small. All that's needed is a partner or three to five persons max. The bigger the group, the more difficult it is to keep everyone on the same page.

Study with friends but add others. Often friends share the same major, gender, and race; ergo, they tend to think alike. Those with other perspectives see things from a different angle, offer alternative explanations, and suggest new examples. This deepens understanding.

Meet more often and for shorter periods of time. Marathon study sessions are less effective than shorter sessions held regularly. Encourage those in the group to schedule some sessions between exams and then several to prepare for the exam.

Prepare an agenda and expect group members to come prepared. Decide beforehand what will be studied the next session and what group members need to do to come prepared. Don't allow freeloaders and be firm with group members who arrive unprepared.

Use good study strategies. Explain things to each other. Ask each other questions. Do problems. Work to understand the content.

Strategies to avoid. Don't "go over" the notes or readings. "Get into" them. Don't just re-read class notes or text material. Don't recopy notes. Don't memorize things that are not understood.

REFERENCE

McCabe, J. A. and Lummis, S. N. (2018). Why and how do undergraduates study in groups? *Scholarships of Teaching and Learning in Psychology, 4* (1), 27-42.

Student-Run Study Groups: A Model

Most teachers endorse study groups. They correctly believe that if students in the group used good study strategies that would help them learn and improve their exam scores. Most teachers don't have time to organize or supervise study groups, especially in large classes where they may be most needed.

H. J. Robinson (*The Teaching Professor*, May, 1991) outlined a model for student run study groups. His approach divests teachers of most of the responsibility for managing them. Here's an adapted version of the guidelines he proposed. Students on commuter campuses should be encouraged to consider online study groups.

- Groups of 4–6 students are formed by the mutual agreement of the members. Or, the teacher could help students interested in a study groups connect with each other.

- To be considered a study group in the course, groups must register with the instructor, providing group member names and contact information.

- Groups may expel a member (say one who is using the group as opposed to contributing to it) by unanimous vote. Students who'd like to join an already existing group, may ask to join. The group decides if they are welcome.

- If group membership falls below four, the group is automatically disbanded unless they find and agree upon a replacement.

- No students may belong to more than one study group and no student is required to belong to any study group.

- Groups organize their own activities, deciding what to do at their meetings. The Handout for Students Interested in Studying with Others (in this section) offers advice on forming and running study groups. The instructor may volunteer to meet with groups to suggest activities and/or to review proposed study plans. The list of Test Review Activities (find it in Section 2) could be shared with groups. Group meetings with the instructor (during regular office hours) are optional.

- Registered groups receive exam bonus points according to the following formula: The bonus is based on the average of all individual grades received by the group members. If the group average is with the A range, all members receive three percentage points; if it's B, two percentage points, and if it's a C one percentage point. If an individual member receives an A but the group average is C, the member still receives the one percentage point bonus.

Ways to Encourage Students to Study Together

Studying together doesn't work when students saunter into study sessions, mostly not on time, sit around, check phones, and socialize. When they finally start reviewing their notes, the text, or the homework problems, if all they do is ask each other a few questions and discuss how hard/easy the course is, then they're wasting time. Also without much value are those conversations reporting what they from others about the exam. They'd like to be persuaded that the test will be easy. Perhaps this explains why only 42 percent of students in one study participated in study groups for exam preparation and only 18 percent found them valuable. [Andaya, G., Hrabak, V., Reyes, S., Diaz, R. and McDonald, K. (2017). Examining the effectiveness of a postexam review activity to promote self-regulation in introductory biology students. *Journal of College Science Teaching*, 46 (4), 84-92.]

If students studied more seriously, many (maybe closer to most) of them would benefit enormously. Working with others provides a safe place to ask questions, to admit confusion or the failure to understand. Often, it's easier for students to understand each other than the teacher. And when students explain things to each other, the student doing the explaining comes to a deeper understanding. When students figure out things on their own, that builds confidence.

What students need when they study together is guidance and the teacher can provide that without taking on the time-consuming task of organizing and managing study groups. Here's some examples of the kind of guidance teachers can provide.

Encourage students to study together

- Make the case for study groups—why and how they improve exam performance for most students.

- Solicit endorsements of study groups from current or former students. Post those on the course website, include them in the syllabus or put them on review materials you prepare for students.

- Demonstrate the benefits by using groups during in-class review. See the list of activities below for ideas.

- Let students form the groups and figure out the logistics: who, how many, and meeting times, including frequency and length. Even one study buddy is better than none.

- Offer to connect students who'd like to study with others.

- Emphasize studying together as part of exam preparation for one exam, challenging students to see if the group supports and helps their study efforts.

- Encourage students to consider online study groups

Provide a list of study group activities. Use these to generate a list that work with your content and for your students.

- Generate potential exam questions or problems—Each group member works with a chunk of content, preparing possible test questions or problems which the group uses to test their knowledge and understanding.

- Facilitated discussion of notes—Each group member is responsible for one or more class session(s). They lead the group's discussion of that content, identifying what's most important, where there's related material in the text, and how that content fits with other material that's been covered. This works best if the group meets once a week or once every two weeks as opposed to once just before the exam.

- Preparation of study materials—Each group member gets a section of text or set of problems and prepares review materials or problem solutions for the rest of the group. Each group member could discuss the content covered in the materials they've prepared.

- Grade answers—Provide groups with sample essay question answers and let students "grade" them with the discussion generating grading criteria for essay answers.

- What's going to be on the test?—The group constructs of list of content areas, concepts or details that everyone agrees they'll need to know for the exam.

Offer guidelines that make study sessions productive.

- Distribute the Study Groups Handout for Students from this section. Be welcome to revise it.

- Members arrive on time; the session starts and ends on time.

- Students get together regularly for shorter sessions.

- There's an agenda; members have decided beforehand what the group will be doing.

- Group members come prepared. Everyone is expected to contribute. Those who don't are constructively confronted.

- The group doesn't waste time. Socializing, phone checking and other disruptive actions are kept to a minimum. It's about the content.

- Members treat each other with respect; no one is demeaned when they are confused or not understanding.

- There's a spirit of sharing. People help each other out.

- Members do what the group needs. If the discussion is off track, someone gets the group back on task. If someone is not contributing, their participation is invited.

Possible incentives

- If everyone in the group scores above a certain level, everyone in the groups gets a designated number of points.

- Make study group participation an optional, extra credit assignment. Groups must register with you, report on their sessions (who was there, what they did), and each member writes a short paper after the exam, reflecting on their experience. If all that happens, it counts for a designated amount of extra credit.

- Groups may submit potential exam questions. Those that show up on the exam are identified as group questions, and if everyone in the group get the question correct, they get a bonus point.

- Let officially registered, regularly meeting groups take one of the quizzes as a group with everyone getting the group grade.

- If groups are officially registered, calculate an exam average for the groups and compare that with the overall exam average.

- Give a student who's doing well in the course the option of leading a study group. Let that activity replace a course assignment.

Study Groups: They Can Improve Grades and Learning

A HANDOUT FOR STUDENTS INTERESTED IN STUDYING WITH OTHERS

Students can learn from and with each other—that's supported by multitudes of research and maybe in your own experience as well. The learning doesn't happen automatically, and the group study doesn't rule out the necessity of individual study. But study groups can improve exam scores and deepen students' understanding of the content. Based on that research, here's a set of guidelines that improve the effectiveness of study groups. I encourage you to share them with your students.

Size—Smaller is better than larger, all the way down to one study buddy. In general, avoid groups greater than seven. Four to six members is a good range.

Group composition—Invite classmates you can trust and communicate with comfortably, but also add some diversity to the group—not all the same majors, for example. Students in the same major tend to think alike, and there's a benefit to hearing something explained, or a question asked by somebody who approaches the content differently. Ditto for some group members with different experience sets, different perspectives, and different backgrounds.

Meet more than once—It takes time for a group to gel, but the real reason is the effectiveness of short, regular study periods. Yes, cramming does work in some courses, but if the content is something you care about or if exams are cumulative, it makes sense to get the group together several times—for say 30 minutes every other week or 30 minutes three times the week before the exam, as opposed to two hours the night before the test.

Group dynamics matter—How group members feel about the effectiveness of the group is largely determined by how well the group functions. How the members want the group to operate should be discussed up front: we'll arrive on time, start and end on time, we'll know what we're going to review before hand, we'll come prepared, and we'll all contribute. If those are the rules and someone doesn't live up to them, the group can decide whether they should be asked to leave. Individuals in a group have the right to expect the group to function productively and the group has the right to expect individual members to function productively.

Good group study strategies—There's excellent research on study strategies that make a difference in exam performance. Unfortunately, a lot of favorite study strategies don't cut the mustard. Groups should focus on those study strategies that are more difficult to do when studying alone. Here's a run-down of dos and don'ts:

- Don't "go over" content; "get into" it. Don't spend time talking about how the exam will be easy and or sharing hearsay about the exams in this course.

- Going over content means a quick and easy discussion of it. Getting into it means taking a concept, explaining it to the group, and providing relevant examples. Getting into it means checking what's in your notes against what's in the text or other assigned readings.

- Do use the study group to improve your class notes. Take a day and have everyone discuss what they've got in their notes. Or, assign each group member a class session and have them give everyone in the group a copy of their notes, elaborated with references to related material in the text.

- Asking and answering potential test questions is a very effective group study strategy. Do consider having everyone bring two or three possible test questions or problems and then use the time together to come up with answers. Yes, it's easier to just talk about the content, but that's not what you'll be doing on the exam, so try to replicate the exam experience as much as possible. It's more difficult and it can be embarrassing, because it makes clear what you don't know or understand. Better find that out in the group than on the exam. And chances are good, there'll be someone in the group who does understand and can explain it to you.

Touch bases after the exam—Not necessarily to share scores, but to chat about what the group contributed to exam preparation. Should the group continue? If so, what if anything, might the group do that would better support individual study?

And finally, don't be shy about asking your classmates join you in a study group. You can start small, just two or three persons you know. Or, post an invite online and don't rule out the possibility of an online study group. Set up the first meeting and start by asking everyone how they think a study group might help with exam preparation in this course.

REVIEW AND REFLECTION

WORKSHEET 1

Here's a set of questions about study groups and whether they might play a larger role in helping your students master course material. It's good to remember as you reconsider materials in this section that learning in groups doesn't happen automatically. Students may need help identifying effective approaches for group study as well as advice on managing group logistics.

1. How many of your students do study with others in your courses? Have you asked? What are they doing when they get together to study?

2. Have you recommended study groups to your students? What advice on forming and managing those groups would be helpful to your students?

3. Would you be willing incentive study group activities in some of the ways suggested in the resources?

4. Are there some ways you could collect evidence that study group in your courses improve exam performance? If you collect evidence and find that they don't, how would you explain that result?

5. Given the nature of your content, what aspects of it need to be mastered individually and what parts of it benefit from exploration with others?

REFLECTION, ACTION, AND RESULTS

WORKSHEET 2

REFLECTION

Resources in the section made me think about these points differently, or, my biggest take away from this section was...

ACTION

❑ I plan to gather information about the use of study groups in my courses. I will survey students, invite commentary online and talk individually with selected students.

❑ I will design a model study group; how many members, member characteristics, number of meetings, study activities, ways to handle group dynamics and group assessment. I will share the model with students.

❑ I plan to regularly encourage use of study groups. I will provide that encouragement by:

1. _____

2. _____

3. _____

RESULTS

Here's my plan for assessing the actions I'm planning to take:

After taking those actions, I've seen these differences in my students, their learning and my teaching:

STUDYING FOR EXAMS

Introduction

Most students study for exams or at least aspire to. Some of those who study do well. Some (generally more than a few) don't study very diligently and others put in the effort but don't get the results. Bottom line: most students have a lot to learn about studying for exams. As the research highlighted in Section 1: Students and Studying: What We Know indicates some of students' favorite study strategies have little or no empirical support.

Most all of us offer students advice on how to study for exams. We tell them to start early, to come to class, to keep up with the reading, to do the homework problems, to ask questions and admit when they're confused. But too often that good advice falls on deaf ears. The resources in this section deliver the how-to study advice in different formats. But the place to study is with accurate information about (not impressions of) how students prepare for exams. Teachers need to know that and so do students. Are they devoting more or less time to exam preparation than is needed to perform well? And what are they doing when they study? There's a question set included in the resources that can be used to create a survey, the answers to which will reveal how students study for exams.

Do students develop a game plan for how they intend to study for an exam? Most of them have some general ideas about what they hope to do but not a specific plan. Getting them to make those details concrete gives them a benchmark against which to measure how they did study and what sort of exam results that produced. In fact, there's an interesting assignment described where students tried various study strategies and assessed their effectiveness. It's not an assignment that can be used in every course, but parts of it could.

As documented in Students and Studying: What We Know (page 71), students aren't all that knowledgeable about evidence-based study strategies. Perhaps you verified that if you had them take the study strategies quiz included in that section. Or, you might use the memo in this section that concisely lays out those strategies and challenges students to try them. Students need to discover what strategies work well for them, not by thinking about them, but by actually putting them to the test.

When students study, they tend to be very answered focused. Their default approach regularly involves memorizing answers. If they're asked lower order questions, ones that can be answered with factoids, they'll do okay, but if the questions make them think, memorized answers aren't much help. What works much better than memorizing answers are potential test questions—what students think they will be asked and how they'd answer those questions. That approach to studying is more work but it's also way more effective. There are some ideas on student generated test questions in the section—approaches that get them involved in coming up with potential test questions and answers.

And finally, there's a couple of resources here (and several in Developing Students' Understandings of Themselves as Learners, page 135) that confront students with how they studied for an exam and their performance on it. Students need disavow themselves of the belief that that they somehow "lucked out" and got a good score, or that they didn't because the test "wasn't fair." Exam wrappers are an approach some teachers use but there are also some alternatives that require more in-depth analysis.

Most students care about exams first and foremost in terms of the grades they generate, but that concern can be used to promote more accurate understandings of those studying strategies shown to positively influence performance and learning.

How Do You Study for an Exam?

Here's a set of questions that could be used to find out how your students study for exams. You'll find another set of questions about how students study in Students and Studying: What We Know, page 7. Those questions focus on studying for the course more generally. These questions focus on how students study for an exam are drawn from a number of sources and reworded here for consistency. There are options to consider and decision to make before using them.

- Do you want to know how students studied for a particular exam in your course, how they've studied for exams taken so far in the course or in general how students study for exams?

- What questions should you ask? These questions touch on a wide range of study behaviors. Which are most relevant given the content of your course and the type of exam you use? Which are of most interest to you? Could you let students identify some of the questions that are of interest to them?

- How do you want students to answer, with closed or open-ended questions? The statements below can be answered yes/no or you could use a Likert-type scale with numbers or descriptors such as; very often, often, sometimes, rarely or never. You make the questions open-ended, for example, what do you do when you get a wrong answer on a homework problem? Or, how do you study the notes you've taken in class. You could add one or two open-ended questions at the end of the survey: If you could improve one thing about how you study, what would you improve? What can the teacher do to better support your efforts to study?

- How do you want to collect and analyze the data? Use something like Survey Monkey or a feature of your local LMS?

- What will you do with the results? Use them to enlarge your understanding of how students study? Share and discuss the results with students, in class or online? Sharing the results with students allows them to benchmark their behavior against their peers in the course. You could collect responses from students doing well in the course and then use those results in subsequent courses so that students have accurate information as how much and what kind of study it takes to do well in the course.

- Will you make changes based on the results? If so, what will you change and how? If students identify some teacher actions that would better support their efforts to learn, and you provide some of those, research indicates that's very motivating to students. So if they asked for an in-class review session before the exam and you provide it, they would likely show up and be ready to review.

HOW DO YOU STUDY FOR AN EXAM?

STUDENT QUESTIONNAIRE

1. When you study for an exam, you study the notes you have taken in class.

2. When you study for an exam, you study the notes, slides and handout materials the teacher has provided

3. When you study your notes for an exam, you copy the notes over.

4. When you study your notes for an exam, you reorganize the notes, make them into outlines, look at definitions and try to put them in your words.

5. When you begin preparing for an exam, you set up a schedule and identify how much material you'll review each time you study.

6. If the content you are studying for the test is confusing, you review your notes and look for additional information in the text.

7. If content you are studying for the test is confusing, you talk to a colleague who is taking or has taken the course.

8. If you're struggling with lots of course content before the test, you head to the Learning Center for help.

9. If you have questions or need help preparing for the exam, you come and talk to the prof during office hours.

10. When you study for an exam you reread our notes.

11. When you study for an exam you review assigned readings that you've already read.

12. When you study for an exam you reread material in the text you've highlighted.

13. You prepare for exams (review notes, do the homework problems, read the text) between the exams, reviewing various materials several times a week.

14. You study for the exam materials with a buddy or in a study group.

15. When you study for an exam, you use flashcards.

16. You talk to students who have taken the course previous to ask what's on the tests.

17. You talk to student who have taken the course previously to get advice on the best ways to study for course exams.

18. If you receive a disappointing grade, one that you didn't expect, you talk to the professor and see if you can figure out what happened.

19. When you are studying for an exam, you minimize distractions (turning off electronic devices, studying in a quiet place).

20. When studying for an exam, you ask yourself potential exam questions and try to answer them without looking at your notes or the text.

21. When studying an exam [in this course or generally] you usually spend [fill in what you think is an appropriate amount] hours.

22. When studying for an exam [in this course or generally] you usually start studying exam [fill in what you think is an appropriate amount] day(s) before the test.

A STUDY GAME PLAN ASSIGNMENT FOR STUDENTS

ASSIGNMENT DESCRIPTION:

Part 1—In two weeks we have our first exam in the course. Develop a game plan that describes how you plan to study for that exam. Use the following prompts to prepare your plan which you'll submit before our next class session.

1. What study strategies will you use to prepare for the exam?

2. What content are you expecting you will need to know for the exam?

3. What about a timeline? How long do you plan to study? How much time do you anticipate you will need to devote to studying in order to do well on the exam?

4. Make a guess about your grade: not the one you want, the one you expect you'll get.

5. Make a good faith effort to develop a reasonably detailed study plan, submit it on time and get full credit.

Part 2—After the exam has been graded and returned, revisit your game plan and prepare a one-page typed response. Be honest. If you do the assignment, you'll get full credit so there's no need to impress me with how much you studied or how hard you tried. Address these prompts in your response

1. How closely did you follow your game plan? Be specific, if you said you'd study five hours, how many hours did you study?

2. Assess the effectiveness of the study strategies you used? Any that worked well? Any that didn't help all that much?

3. What about your expected grade and the one you got? Close, not so close? Why?

4. What about the next exam? This game plan, a revision of this one or a totally new approach—what's your plan?

Submit this response on time with the prompts addressed and you've earned full credit.

I used this assignment (I've made it a bit more generic here) in most of my introductory courses. I was always a bit surprised by the number of students who indicated this was the first time they'd ever developed a study game plan for an exam—not all of these were beginning students. I tried to drive home the value of doing so with an athletic metaphor. "Would you go into a big game without having thought about the opponent and the best way to play against them? Wouldn't you devise some sort of game plan for practice and for the game itself?"

I was also impressed by how much students proposed to study and then how little they actually did. Maybe the timelines they developed were created to impress me or was that how much time they really believed they needed to study? As for the grade they expected to earn, generally only about 10 percent were within three points of their actual score. The vast majority of the rest wildly over estimated their grade.

I didn't grade the assignment for the propriety of the student's plan. I wanted them to be honest, mostly with themselves. And I think most were. Lots of them readily conceded they would have done much better had they followed the plan they'd devised. They were less insightful about the study strategies they'd used. Students who'd done poorly—whose strategies had not prepared them for the exam—didn't question their choices. Instead they said they needed to do more of what they did. That wasn't always a bad answer—reviewing notes from class more and spending more time studying the text would improve the scores of most. But if making flashcards didn't help with the vocabulary, is continued use of them a good option? I discovered in conversations with students some of them couldn't change study strategies because they weren't aware of other options.

I wish I'd had students do this assignment for every exam. It confronted them with a number of activities they hadn't done previously; develop a study plan, note the strategies they intended to use, assess their effectiveness and confront grade over estimations with an explanation. The assignment illustrates an approach that can lead to some important insights.

A Study-for-an-Exam Assignment

To remediate the exam preparation study skills that beginning (and other) students are missing, most of us respond by telling students about those behaviors and skills that result in good exam performance. "Come to class." "Take notes." "Keep up with reading." "See me during office hours if you need help." And most of us have discovered that this approach isn't particularly effective. First, students tend not to listen all that closely to advice on how to study when it's offered by persons who sound and often look like parents, and second, it's not enough to know what they should be doing. Students have to use those skills.

Here's an approach that might succeed where how-to-study admonitions fail. It starts with a first-year seminar program which provides a perfect structure for this assignment but is not absolutely essential. In this first-year seminar course students get the usual instruction on learning strategies, but more importantly they complete an assignment in the seminar called a Strategy Project Assignment. It's a "multistep project requiring students to plan, monitor, and evaluate their newly learned strategies as they prepare for a test in a course in which they are currently enrolled." (pp. 272-3)

A copy of the actual assignment appears in an appendix at the end of the article referenced below. It includes students creating a study game plan, meeting with the instructor about the exam, using the reading review activities that have been covered in the course, using active note-taking strategies, implementing a choice of appropriate exam study strategies, taking the test, predicting the grade and then once the test is returned writing a paper the reflects on their exam preparation and performance. Evidence that all these activities were completed is required and they are evaluated to determine the overall assignment grade.

This is another of those "authentic assignments" where students do work that requires the application and use of course content. It relies on what's called "deliberative practice." "In order for a person to achieve mastery levels, practice of the skill in an authentic context is necessary." (p. 272)

An analysis of the reflection papers students (in five seminar sections) wrote after the exam revealed five themes.

The first and "perhaps most important" (p. 274) theme involved the value students placed on the assignment and this was after initial reactions that weren't all that enthusiastic. "This project has to be the most eye-opening project of my entire semester," one student wrote (p. 274)

Second, students commented on the transition from high school to college and their vague expectations of what doing well in college required. They knew they were going to have to work harder. Even so, some felt confident. One admitted to feeling "cocky." Other were fearful, convinced they were going to fail. Either way, their expectations tended to be inaccurate.

Many also wrote about their reluctance to change what had worked in high school. They didn't want to use the strategies being proposed in the seminar. They didn't think they would work. What they'd done in high school worked, why should they change?

But the new strategies the assignment forced them to use did work. Forty-five percent of the students reported a letter grade or higher increase on the test they prepared for in the project. Another 26 percent reported smaller improvement gains. The few that reported declines attributed them to personal circumstances, not the project.

Perhaps more significant that grade gains were the changes in self-efficacy that resulted from the assignment. Another regular theme addressed how much more confident students felt about taking exams. They described feeling prepared and able to handle exam questions. And finally, many of the students reported that the assignment had caused them to make permanent changes in how they prepare for exams across the board.

An assignment like this is perfectly suited for a first-year seminar course, but as the author points out, it can be adapted for use in a variety of courses, most appropriately in those regularly taken by beginning students or in those courses where the approaches students tend to use are not the ones that result in good grades and successful learning. The assignment could also work well in those first courses in a major where students need to learn the ins and outs of studying a particular kind of content.

It's not an assignment that can be used in all courses, but it's not needed in every course. This works shows the value of having it one course.

REFERENCE

Steiner, H. H., (2016). The strategy project: Promoting self-regulated learning through an authentic assignment. *International Journal of Teaching and Learning in Higher Education, 28* (2), 271-282.

MEMO TO STUDENTS

To: My Students

From: Your Teacher

Re: Studying for exams

No, this isn't the usual plea urging you to study more. This is about getting you to think about what you do when you study. Based on lots of evidence, researchers can tell you which approaches are the most likely to improve exam scores. Do you know how you should study?

Would you like to venture some guesses? From my vantage point, I'd say students have three favorite study strategies: highlighting, re-reading, and cramming. Brightly colored highlighters in hand, students highlight key passages—you might highlight most of a page if you aren't sure what's important—and when you study, you re-read those passages. When I ask about exam preparation, you tell me you're going to "go over" (as in re-read) your notes. And we all know students cram for exams. You don't intend to cram, but lives are busy and there are many more pressing or interesting options than studying. So, it's the night before the exam or the hour before the test, and you're shoveling material fast and furiously in the direction of your head. Are those the most effective study strategies? Not according to the researchers. In fact, highlighting, re-reading, and cramming are at the bottom of their lists.

What's at the top? Practice testing. Now, that doesn't mean getting an old test from the course, looking at the right answers, and hoping the test doesn't change from semester to semester. It means looking at those test questions and trying to answer them on your own, doing the same thing with the chapter study questions, or studying with a buddy and asking each other potential test questions. Most students turn up their noses at this strategy because it's more work, but it's so much more effective than reviewing your notes. You can re-read something and convince yourself you understand it because it seems familiar. It's not until you try to answer questions about it that you see just how deep (or shallow) your understanding is. Sure, it takes more time and effort, but it's better to find out before the test than during it. The reason practice testing works: You're doing what you're going to be doing on the exam—answering questions!

What else works? Regular review, not cramming and not marathon study sessions. Yes, cramming does work. Students wouldn't have done it for decades if it didn't produce results. But here's the rub when it comes to cramming. It's fine if the test questions ask you to regurgitate bits and pieces of information, those memorized details that you've temporarily stashed upstairs. If the question asks you to put that information together or apply it to something new and all you've got are information bytes, you're in trouble. The second problem is that even with a respectable exam score, you haven't learned what the grade says you know. Two weeks later, you can't take that exam and get the same score. Regular review provides more opportunities to retrieve the material, which makes it that much easier to understand and remember.

The research is also pretty clear that students can learn from each other. Students can explain things to each other in a language they understand and with examples that make sense to them. Students can ask each other "stupid" questions—ones they'd rather not ask the teacher. In some situations, I think students can learn better from each other than from the teacher. When someone has studied a content area for a long time, it's hard to remember what it's like not knowing the basics. The concepts seem simple, obvious and teachers can't figure out why students are confused. But a fellow classmate who's just learned it out knows exactly why it's hard, confusing, and doesn't make sense. So, get yourself a study buddy or consider forming a study group.

I'm a bit concerned about research that shows how reluctant students are to change how they study. Really? It is true that students learn in different ways so not every approach works equally well for every person. But this is college, the place you go to get prepared for lifelong learning and to discover new perspectives, so find out what study strategies work best for you! And don't settle for what you "think" is best. Try out some new study strategies. If you're worried about doing that on an exam, try them out on a quiz. See if they make a difference in your performance and in how well you understand what you're learning.

And lastly, I am here to help. Learning is hard, messy work but you've got me on your side and I'm committed to helping you make it happen.

Study Strategies Students Use for Exam Preparation

Here's a set of behaviors and activities that have been shown to improve exam performance. Many of them are common sense; but a lot of them aren't regularly used by students. Some of the most widely used strategies are ones that have been shown not to improve exam performance or for which there is no or inconclusive evidence. Those appear on the second list.

The lists could be used this way: combine them and have students indicate which of the activities they plan to use as part of their exam preparation. Encourage them to be realistic and identify the approaches they are most likely to use. You could collect and compile the results. When you return the exam, attach a second copy of the list. At that point students rate the effectiveness of the strategies they used. In a follow-up discussion you might share class averages and divulge that not all the strategies on the list are evidence based.

Sometimes students stick with the strategies they know because they don't know or haven't seriously considered alternatives. This approach may get them to modify how they prepare for exams.

Study strategies shown to improve test performance

- Regular class attendance

- Review of teacher provided materials; notes, PowerPoint slides, handouts

- Do readings as they're assigned

- Do homework problems, answering them before looking up the answer

- Take hand written notes in class

- Study by asking potential test questions, answer them before looking up the answers

- Study course materials regularly between exams

- Take the quizzes seriously; prepare for them

- Study course materials for short periods

- Mix up course materials and/or problems, study them in a different than they were presented

- Study with a buddy or participate in a study group

- Review notes possibly reordering them, rewrite definitions and content using language that clarifies the meaning

- Attend review sessions

Strategies without research support

- Do assigned readings just before the exam

- Go over (as in reread) class notes

- Highlighting lots important material in the text

- Look over highlighted text material when studying for the exam

- Memorize definitions and details even if they aren't understood

- Talk to others about the test; will it be hard/easy, what kinds of questions to expect

The behaviors and activities on these lists are drawn from a variety of sources. The two below are good summaries of the research that's been done on approaches to learning.

REFERENCES

Dunlosky, J., Rawson, K. A., Marsh, E. J., Nathan, M. J. and Willingham, D. T., (2013). Improving student's learning with effective learning techniques: Promising directions from cognitive and educational psychology. *Psychological Science in the Public Interest, 14* (1), 4-58.

Chew, S., (2014). How to help student get the most out of studying. In Benassi, V. A., Overson, C. E., & Hakala, C. M. (Editors). (2014). Applying science of learning in education: Infusing psychological science into the curriculum. Retrieved from the Society for the Teaching of Psychology website: http://teachpsych.org/ebooks/asle2014/index.php

Student-Generated Test Questions

When studen`ts study for exams, they tend to be focused on answers. They aren't thinking about questions. But thinking up questions expedites learning the answers. It's the essential first step in using test-enhanced learning, that research tested study strategy with well-established positive results. [See the collection of study strategy resources in Section 1: Students and Studying: What We Know to review the evidence on test-enhanced learning.]

Those who've used this strategy all agree that students need help learning how to write test questions. Don't use this strategy if you aren't willing to take some class time to work on those skills or to provide resources (like handouts with guidelines and examples) that students can use to develop the skills on their own. Writing good test questions is hard work and most students don't have much experience writing them.

There's also agreement that this is an activity that has the potential to engage students. They care about test questions. So, if you work with them, say during the last five minutes of class to generate a potential test questions, that not only provides a good review of the content, it can also clarify student thinking about the kinds of questions they should expect to find on the test.

You can go further with this strategy. Here's an example of how it can become an assignment with student generated questions actually showing up on the exam. When students understand that's may happen option, their interest in generating potential test questions grow exponentially

A Test-Question Generation Assignment

Marketing professor Donna Green, who developed this assignment, provides students advice on writing test questions—in this case multiple-choice and short answer questions—when she first makes the assignment. In her experience this step is key and cannot be omitted. Her article includes the guidelines she gives students on writing multiple-choice questions (p. 50).

All the student generated questions and answers are entered into an instructor database. When entering the question, she rates them for difficulty and includes the question type, topic area, student's name, source of the question, and its cognitive level. As soon as possible after a topic has been covered and the questions submitted, all the questions but not their answers are made available to students.

When Green constructs course exams, she chooses student questions that cover the content and that are at different cognitive levels. She does edit student questions if they are poorly worded, too easy, or too hard. She also makes sure that each student is the author of at least one question on the exam. She adds questions she has written to cover material students may have missed and questions that tend to require more analysis and synthesizing than the students' questions. She does not provide more than 25 percent of the questions on the exam.

Her article discusses both the advantages and disadvantages of this assignment which student respond to positively. Green notes that good questions cannot be written without serious interaction with course concepts and terminology. She also notes that student-generated questions make "the examinations interesting for both students and professor. Some students are quite creative and can write excellent questions that go right to the heart of the important issues." (p. 48) Her students like seeing questions attributed to them on the exam, and everyone knows there is at least one question on the exam they are guaranteed to get right. Most of the disadvantages involve the time required to manage the assignment details.

For even more details on this assignment as well as a nice review of the literature on student test question generation check out this article.

REFERENCE

Green, D. H., (1997). Student-generated exams: Testing and learning. *Journal of Marketing Education, Summer, 43-53.*

And from Someone who Tried this Approach

Sometime after I highlighted Green's article in the *Teaching Professor*, Edward Venckus wrote a follow-up piece describing his experiences using Green's approach. His students submitted between 7–10 multiple-choice questions per unit which he graded as "ok" or "not acceptable" for five percent of students' course grade. The best 4–8 questions for each unit he posted, and like Green, he identified the question's author. For the midterm and the final, these student generated questions constituted 10 percent of the exam items. Venckus recommends that teachers implement the strategy, one course at a time because of the time investment required. His students also responded positively to the assignment. He describes it as "extremely valuable for getting students involved in review prior to major exams."

—Venckus' article appears in the August/September, 1999 issue of *The Teaching Professor*.

Exam Wrappers

The exam wrapper is a strategy that encourages students to confront the connection between how they prepared for the exam and how they performed on it. It's been proposed and used in a variety of formats, with some of the effects studied empirically. Basically the "wrapper" is attached to the exam with students answering the questions after they've completed the exam. Often, there's a second set of questions answered when or after the exam is returned.

Consider the before and after questions on the exam wrapper offered here as examples. Be welcome to use any of them but also be welcome to revise, replace and otherwise modify them to fit the particulars of your exams. Should you offer bonus points to encourage thoughtful responses? That's a question you'll need to answer. It's an option and if it does encourage students to take the activity more seriously, it may be worth a few points.

I'd recommend taking a look at the wrappers and sharing at least some of the results with students. One option is to use the results to generate a list of recommended study strategies, perhaps focusing on those used by students who did well on the exam.

Another option is to collect the second set of exam wrappers responses and return them to students before the next exam. Finally, some faculty make the exam wrappers an ongoing activity. They are part of every exam experience and in that case can be used to keep students focused on improvement efforts.

EXAM WRAPPER

Instructions to students: Please answer these questions when you've finished taking the exam. There's a second set you'll answer when the exam is returned to you. The goal is to provide you and me important feedback on the exam. Your answers will not in any way influence the grade you've earned on the test. So, please be honest with me and yourself. Carefully thought answers to the two questions sets will earn you five bonus points. These bonus points are not dependent on you saying you studied hard or that it was a good exam.

QUESTIONS TO BE ANSWERED AFTER TAKING THE EXAM.

1. Did you prepare a study game plan before you started studying for the exam? Briefly describe what you planned to do.

2. How much time did you spend preparing for this exam?

3. List the days you studied for the exam and the amount of time spent on each of these days?

4. What percentage of your study time was spent on each of these activities?

    _____ reading the textbook for the first time

    _____ reviewing material in the textbook

    _____ reviewing previously assigned homework problems

    _____ working new practice problems

    _____ reviewing notes taken in class

    _____ rewriting notes taken in class

    _____ testing your knowledge with possible test questions

    _____ working on course content with a study buddy or in a study group

    _____ looking over material provided on the course website

    _____ reviewing instructor provided test questions

    _____ writing out answers to potential short answer/essay questions

5. How closely did you follow your study game plan?

6. List the number(s) of the test questions you could not answer but had to guess.

7. List the number(s) of any test questions where you did not understand the question.

8. Predict your score on the exam.

9. Was the exam harder, easier or just about what you expected?

QUESTIONS TO BE ANSWERED AFTER YOU'VE REVIEWED YOUR GRADED EXAM

1. If there is more than a three-point difference between your exam score and the score you predicted, how would you explain the difference?

2. Assess the effectiveness of the study strategies you relied on most? Which do you plan to continue using? Are there any that did not help your exam performance?

3. Based on this exam, list what, if anything, you plan to do differently for the next exam.

4. If you do the things just identified, how much improvement would you expect to see in your exam score?

5. What, if anything, could we be doing in class that would contribute to your efforts to prepare for the next exam?

Confronting Exam Performance: Learning from how I Studied

In most cases, telling students how they should study for exams doesn't seem to have much effect on their behavior. They have their ways of studying which worked well in high school so that's what they continue to try use in college. Favero and Hendricks believe that students must confront those less than effective approaches and that an analysis of exam results can provide insights and motivate behavior changes. They designed an activity that promotes a constructive encounter with exam results and exam preparation strategies, and it doesn't involve class time.

"Despite the fact that the cognitive tasks in college multiply and diversify, students generally apply their similar study techniques across multiple disciplines until those techniques no longer produce adequate results," observe Favero and Hendricks (p. 325). They decided the time to confront study strategy issues was as part of the exam debrief. In two sections of a human anatomy course taken mostly by biology and nursing students, students were invited to debrief their exam during the professor's office hours, any time before the second exam. Fifty-two percent of the students accepted the invitation with the remaining students serving as a control group.

The exam debrief (ED) process consisted of five parts which the students completed before meeting with the professor. The handout given to students is included in the article.

- Part 1—Students look carefully at the questions they missed and see if they can determine why they missed each question.

- Part 2—Then students see if there's a pattern emerging. Are they missing questions for the same reason? Are they missing the same kinds of questions?

- Part 3—The request here is for a brief description of how the student studied for the exam including how much time was spent studying.

- Part 4—Based on the information gleaned so far, students are asked to identify what changes they think they could make that might help them better prepare for the next exam. The handout they are given lists the areas where changes could be made: time on task, attending to detail, using active learning strategies, and general study habits. Examples are given in each of these areas.

After completing this ED analysis students meet briefly with the professor to discuss their "findings."

How did this activity affect scores on the next exam? "A significant difference was observed in the mean increase in exam performance from the first exam to the second exam for those students that conducted the ED. The calculated effect size was 0.48, demonstrating a moderate or medium effect size for the ED." (p. 324)

By far and away the most common reason for missing questions was simply not knowing the basic anatomical information needed to answer or being able to narrow down the answer options but then choosing the wrong one. Interestingly, but perhaps not surprisingly, the most common study strategies these students reported using were passive ones; reading the book, taking notes, and reviewing (as in going over) those materials. Only about 25 percent of students indicated they discussed the material with others in the class and less than 15 percent reported active strategies like taking online quizzes.

In the ED process students select the behavior changes they believe they need to make. One-hundred percent of them selected options from the active learning category, in part, the authors believe because those activities are demonstrated, modeled and used in class. For example, many students reported using flash cards but only as devices that helped them memorize details, like definitions. In class, Favero uses an activity with flashcards that shows students how flash cards can more profitably be used to show relationships between, in this case, structure and function.

Did specific study behaviors account for the improvement in exam scores or was that improvement the result of participation in the whole process? The data collected here do not answer that question. It could in fact be the more general approach of putting students in charge a process through which they encountered themselves as learners that garnered these positive results. Whatever the cause, it's an interesting exploration of an approach that directly involves students in a debrief process from which they stand to learn more about effective exam preparation.

REFERENCE

Favero, T. G. and Hendricks, H., (2016). Student exam analysis (debriefing) promotes positive changes in exam preparation and learning. *Advances in Physiology Education, 40* (3), 323-328.

REVIEW AND REFLECTION

WORKSHEET 1

This round of questions encourages you to think more about how students study for your exams and what you might do to improve how they approach exam preparation. The resource collection contains a variety of options which lead to the question of whether you might consider doing more or doing some things differently.

1. What do you know about how your students study for your exams? Do you have impressions or have you collected evidence? What about a quick survey or a focus group conversation? If you record your impressions first, then you compare what they say with what you think.

2. Are your students using evidenced based strategies when they study or do they rely on more generic approaches, like going over their notes and rereading what they've highlighted? How might you challenge them to try some of the more evidence-based approaches?

3. Are you making the most of student interest in exam questions? Do you use them in class? Do you get students involved in generating potential test questions? Have you ever included a student generated question on an exam?

4. Do your students tend to blame the test and excuse themselves when they don't do well? Have you considered constructive ways of encouraging them to confront how they prepared with how they performed?

5. If you could change one thing about how your student study for exams, what would you change? Is that change the one that should be the focus of your attention?

REFLECTION, ACTION, AND RESULTS

WORKSHEET 2

REFLECTION

Resources in the section made me think about these points differently, or, my biggest take away from this section was...

ACTION

❏ I am going to make an effort to find how my students are studying for my exams. I may use some of the survey questions provided in the section. I may do some interviews with students who are doing well in the course and some with those struggling in the course.

❏ I do need to do a better job of sharing information on evidence-based study approaches with my students. Here's several ways I plan to do that:

1. _____

2. _____

❏ Getting students involved in generating potential test questions seems like a good idea to me. Here's how I'm going to try to make that happen in my courses.

1. _____

2. _____

❏ I'm going to encourage my students to start analyzing the test questions they're missing with the goal of trying to figure out kind of questions they are most often missing.

RESULTS

Here's my plan for assessing the actions I'm planning to take:

After taking those actions, I've seen these differences in my students, their learning and my teaching:

Developing Students' Understandings of Themselves as Learners

Introduction

Do your students think of themselves as learners? Or, do they see themselves as students whose job it is to study, do assignments, pass exams, and get good grades? Could they characterize themselves as learners? Do they make decisions about how to study based on understanding how they learn?

Most of our curricula do not provide students many opportunities to encounter themselves as learners. Teachers do regularly encourage students to study and offer advice on effective study strategies which is all well and good, but it's not the kind of information that cultivates an awareness of the self as a learner. As a result, we have a lot of students who aren't confident about themselves learners. They depend on teachers to make the learning decisions for them—how many pages, number of references, and what homework problems they should do. And yet, when students become professionals, they are expected to be self-directed learners, able to manage learning tasks on their own.

This section proposes some ways teachers can begin to cultivate this important awareness of learning. It makes sense to start with students' insights into how they study, those processes they use to learn the content and acquire the skills contained in the course. Those insights can result from activities and assignments—the case in point in this section is a study that highlights an interesting post exam review activity that students conducted on their own and that resulted in important insights and better exam scores.

Sometimes it's hard to see learning progress. Students can become very focused on the ongoing struggles and difficulties in the course. There's still lots of content they don't understand, problems they can't solve, questions they can't answer, and terms with difficult definitions. In those situations, it's easy to forget the content and skills that have been mastered. A resource in this section proposes some before and after assignments and activities where students record what they know about a topic before a learning experience and then revisit that initial understanding after time spent studying it. It's an approach that makes learning visible and that can motivate continued efforts to learn.

A learning log that's a course assignment or a set of learning prompts that student respond to as low-stakes writing options can directly ask about learning experiences and processes. Assignments like these don't require lots of teacher feedback and grading time. Their value derives simply from the process of responding to the prompt and the opportunity it provides to develop more awareness of the self as a learner.

Many course assignments and activities can include a component devoted developing learner awareness. So, after an exam students but before the scores are recorded students send the teacher a memo that identifies what strategies they used to study for the exam and how beneficial were they; a completed paper has a note about the paragraph the student is most proud of and the feedback question the student would most like to have answered; for a short discussion of how participation is occurring in the course, students identify the participation behaviors they would most like to improve and how they might go about improving them. Even small addendums like these prompt students to think about, not just what they are learning, but how they are learning. And out of that attention grows the students' awareness of themselves as learners.

Before and After Learning

Sometimes it isn't all that easy to see that you've learned something or are in the process of doing so. I have sat with many students, handed them something written early in the course, and asked them to look at it in light of something they've just completed. "Do you think your writing has improved?" Invariably they shrug a response, "I don't know." I look and see improvement in almost every sentence.

A recent issue of *Teaching Theology and Religion*, 21, 2), contains an interview with Lynn Neal, the 2017 winner of the American Academy of Religion Excellence in Teaching Award, in which she talks about using "before and after" assignments (p. 143). The assignments struck me as being beneficial on several fronts. First, they can offer students a visible demonstration of learning. You can start a unit asking them to write what they think they know about a topic, then explore that content, and conclude by asking the same question. If students look at what they knew before and after, in most cases, they'll be able to see that they know more.

Even if the learning is still in process, as in a skill that's developing like writing, painting, problem solving, or welding, a before-and-after assessment can make progress visible. The before part may be some low-stakes writing that evaluates skill level, captures all those first-try emotions, and assesses confidence (or lack of it) going forward.

Having this sort of concrete encounter with what has been learned can be very motivational, especially if the content is challenging or the skill is complex. If you don't think you're making progress, discovering accomplishments, even small ones, can provide fuel for continued effort.

Making students more aware of learning as it happens develops several ancillary skills. For example, it helps students more accurately assess their knowledge. "Oh, so I do know that." "Yes, I can do that." Before-and-after writing gives students the opportunity to practice articulating what they know and can do. That process solidifies the knowledge thereby increasing the chance of long-term retention. An awareness of learning grows the appreciation and sometimes love of learning. It also gives students more confidence in their ability to learn, especially when they end up learning or doing something they didn't think they could.

Before-and-after writings—they could also be discussions or in some cases demonstrations—can occur before and after any number of course events: at the beginning and ending of a class session; before and after a course activity or event, say a field trip or guest presenter; before and after an assignment or a collection of assignments; before and after an exam; or at the beginning and ending of the course.

Framing the questions that prompt these kinds of analyses and reflection is important. If students are asked to write what they know about the Kreb Cycle, they'll take care of the request with a single word: nothing. The prompt must encourage students to delve into what they know, think, or might imagine happens to food when it reaches a cell. The prompt needs to encourage students to explore their feelings, not so much about what they're learning, but about the process of learning it. We cannot underestimate the importance of what students believe about their ability as learners. Most of them have strong feelings about what they can and can't do, and those beliefs become barriers to learning. Writing gets those feelings out in the open, and if the learning experience has any positive outcomes—and most do—writing after the fact can raise questions about their beliefs.

If before-and-after writings aren't a required assignment will students take them seriously? You know your students. If you do need to make the assignments worth a few points, let it be low-stakes, where the credit is earned by making an honest effort. If students think points can be earned by calling the learning experience wonderful, that's what many (some, for sure) will do.

Many students don't have a lot awareness of learning. They're so focused on what they're learning, they don't think about it as a process. Anything we can do to increase that awareness further develops their prowess as learners.

Learning Logs

Learning logs can be a great assignment for cultivating the awareness of learning and you can devise a collection of prompts that address a wide range of study beliefs and behaviors. There's a set of prompts below to get you started. They should be tailored to your course content and the learning skills most needed to master that content. Providing prompts is essential to success of a learning log assignment and the more specific the prompt, the better, if especially if your students are early in their college careers. If the assignment too open-ended, students get stuck trying to figure out what you want and that doesn't result in any insights about learning. On the other hand, once students get used to these kinds of prompts and if for some it's an assignment of interest and one that promotes insights, you can give them the chance to write some of their own prompts.

A learning-log assignment can be designed in lots of different ways. It can be big or small, or you can let student determine the size. Provide a collection of prompts and have them select how many and which ones. If you need to prevent the writing a lot of entries all at once, provide smaller groups with a due date and the stipulation that after the deadline responses to those prompts won't be accepted.

Grading learning logs need not be a time-consuming task. Students don't need a lot of feedback. The learning that takes place is more likely a result of the process—it happens as student think and write about what the prompt is asking. A simple rubric that identifies the features of a good-faith effort may be all you need.

Completed logs entries can be used to make points about studying. A response with an insight can be posted anonymously on the course website, read in class or used to open a short discussion of some how-to study related issue.

LEARNING LOG PROMPTS

Select three new terms presented in the course. Define them using definitions presented in class or in the text. Now create definitions using your own words—ones that make sense to you. If examples were presented in class or are in the text, what were those examples? Provide two of your own examples. How does doing this affect your understanding of the terms?

Pick a day in class from a couple of weeks ago. Look at your notes for that day. What are the two or three main points from that class session? Is there anything in your notes that doesn't make sense to you now? See if you can figure it out. Ask someone from class. Check and see if the text has relevant information. Stop by the office and ask me. Write whatever you find out in your log. Overall, how would you assess your ability to figure out things you don't understand?

You'll need a partner for this log entry. Trade notes with your partner. Look over notes your partner took on several different days in class. Jot down some observations about his or her notes. Now compare and contrast your notes and those of your partner. What's the same; what's different? If a conversation with your partner would be helpful, have one.

Look at a couple of pages in your text that you've read recently. Did you highlight anything on those pages? Provide an example of something that you highlighted. How do you decide if you should highlight something? When you're reviewing how do you handle the highlighted material?

Identify something we've covered in class that you think is important but don't really understand at all or very well. Write it down. What do you do when you don't understand some content in a course? What should you do?

When you've finished studying for the first exam in this course, estimate your score and say how confident you are about your estimate. What's the odds that your estimate will be within three points of the actual exam score? When the exam is returned, report your grade. Were you close? If you missed by more than three points, why? How would you explain the difference?

Do you cram for exams, as in spend 75 percent of the time you devoted to studying in the 24 hours before the exam? Does cramming work for you? Why and how well does it work? If you had to take the same exam in two weeks, what would you predict would happen to your score? What if you had to retake an exam you took last semester? How would you do? Does it matter if you forget lots of the material you learned for an exam?

Have you ever taken a course where you learned a lot about learning? What was the course? What did you learn about learning and how did you learn it?

Are there skills you are using to learn the content in this course that you think might be useful in your professional life? What are they and how do you think you might use them?

An Innovative Post-Exam Review Activity

We need to work more with students on seeing exams as something more than just grade generating experiences. Exams can be powerful encounters through which students learn course content and learn about learning. However, given the importance placed on grades, I'm not terribly optimistic about a lot of students discovering on their own what can be learned from an exam experience. We need to frame exams with a stronger focus on learning, and here's a great example.

It's a post-exam review activity originally used in an introductory biology course where the exams were mostly multiple choice. The activity includes these components:

Correcting and Reflecting—With their graded exam returned, students were charged with providing the correct answer for each question missed and identifying the sources they used to correct the answer. Next, they had to explain why their original answer was incorrect. And finally, they had to tell why they missed the question. They did this by selecting from a list of possible reasons—such as misread the question, used incorrect logic, didn't know enough information—or providing an alternative explanation if their reason wasn't listed.

Examining Study Strategies and Behaviors—This component included a list of 16 study tools (e.g. flash cards and concept maps) and behaviors (e.g. regular class attendance and study times). Here students indicated the tools and actions they used to prepare for the exam and which ones they found most helpful.

Using Open–ended Reflection—Finally, students responded to a three-part question: 1) was the grade an accurate reflection of what they knew for the exam and how well prepared they felt; 2) what could they do to improve their learning prior to the next exam; and 3) what could the instructor do to improve their learning experience.

Students had one week after the exam to complete this assignment. It was worth up to 10 points with the exam worth 100 points. Students did the assignment after each of the three major exams, although the structure changed for Exams 2 and 3 to give students more flexibility in their analysis.

What makes this activity especially interesting is the analysis of the assignment undertaken by faculty and students (two are listed as first authors of this piece). The sample size in this first analysis was small, even so the results raise some interesting questions. Not surprisingly, students were able to correct their answers. But when they tried to explain why their incorrect answers couldn't be right, only 62 percent of their responses received a "High Quality" score, using a rubric developed for the analysis. The authors make two points here: students may be able to correct answers and still not understand the material in the exam question; and this discrepancy "underscores a common limitation of multiple-choice questions to accurately assess student understanding." (p. 87)

Students in this sample were also convinced they were using the best methods to prepare for the exam. They relied heavily on materials provided by the instructor—study worksheets and a pre-lecture assignment. Any study approach that required motivation and self-direction, such as self-testing, regular study of the content, reading before attending lecture, were used significantly less often and only 11 percent believed approaches like these held much value, even though the effectiveness of these more self-directed strategies is widely supported by research.

Also, perhaps not surprising, almost half the students didn't feel their grade on Exam 1 reflected what they knew, and they regularly attributed that discrepancy to careless mistakes. "This suggests that they [students] believe using caution is the only measure they need to take to improve their performance on future exams." (p. 90)

Yes, this is a labor-intensive assignment, for teachers and students. Something the authors readily agree. But as the follow-up study reveals, it's an assignment that contributed to improved exam scores and promoted metacognitive development. Students learn the content and they learn more about learning the content. That's a big payoff, and assignments like this don't need to occur in every course. We need to think more strategically about where assignments (of various sorts) should be placed within a curricular experience.

REFERENCES

Andaya, G., Hrabak, V., Reyes, S., Diaz, R. and McDonald, K. (2017). Examining the effectiveness of a postexam review activity to promote self-regulation in introductory biology students. *Journal of College Science Teaching, 46* (4), 84-92.

Dang, N., Chiang, J., Brown, H., and McDonald, K. (2018). Curricular activities that promote cognitive skills impact lower-performing students in an introductory biology course. *Journal of Microbiology and Biology Education, 19* (1), 1-9.

REVIEW AND REFLECTION

WORKSHEET 1

The resources in this section illustrate how free-standing assignments and assignments attached to other course events can be used to cultivate students' awareness of themselves as learners. The questions here ask you to consider what responsibility you may have for promoting these encounters and if you feel it's a responsibility, what you might do about it. Could you add to an activity you current use? Could you incorporate something proposed here?

1. If you asked your students to write a paragraph that described themselves as learners, what do think they might say? What about asking them for the paragraph?

2. Do you ever talk with students about their improvement—what they can do now that they struggled at the beginning of the course? Are they're executing a skill at a different level now? How easy is it for learners to see their improvement? Is seeing improvement important to a learner?

3. Is writing a good way to cultivate learner awareness? Does it work equally well for all learners? If it doesn't, what methods can you use that might help students who don't find their way to personal insights through writing?

4. Does becoming aware of how you learn always result in taking action based on what you know, or is there a disconnect between what you know about how you learn and what you do when you're trying to learn?

5. After taking a look at some or all of these resources in this collection related to developing students as learners, what do you think? Are the resources up to the task? If used will they accomplish the objective?

REFLECTION, ACTION, AND RESULTS

WORKSHEET 2

REFLECTION

Resources in the section made me think about these points differently, or, my biggest take away from this section was…

ACTION

❏ I am going talk with my students about their awareness of themselves as learners. I never have in a purposeful way and I'd like to hear from them if and to what extent they think about themselves as learners.

❏ I plan to add a learner awareness component to a couple of the assignments I'm currently using. Here's the assignments and what I plan to add to them.

1. _____

2. _____

❏ I am going to generate a brief description of what I know about myself as a learner. I'm going to post it on the course website and tell students if they submit a description of how they learn, they can earn up to five bonus points. I will ask them if I may post their descriptions anonymously or with their names on our course website.

RESULTS

Here's my plan for assessing the actions I'm planning to take:

After taking those actions, I've seen these differences in my students, their learning and my teaching:

Conclusion

If I were to conclude by following one of the recurring themes in this collection, I'd have you do the summary! And we wonder why students sometimes resist? It's lots easier to have learning tasks like these done for us. But forcing yourself to think about these resources collectively has benefits. Doing so helps you put the content in a mental space where it's easier to find and unpack.

If you decided to think about a possible summary or the common themes that run through this collection, here's what I'm hoping might come to mind. Teachers can help students develop as learners. It's not impossible, even with all that content that needs to get covered. I tried not to be too overt with the message, but I do think developing these learning skills is part of our responsibility as teachers.

Then there's the message that those skills associated with being an effective and empowered learner develop best when students are given the opportunity to practice them. I don't think students learn them as well by being told how to do them (as in how to study) or by teacher provided examples that showcase the skill (as in always providing the summaries). There's no question that teachers can summarize, review, analyze, explicate, relate, organize, and apply the content better than students can. There's definitely times and places in every course when teachers should do just that. There's also most assuredly times and places in every course when students should be doing that. The skills that develop students as learners are mastered with practice.

I know, often when we see students execute those skills, it makes us flinch. A friend recently sent me a picture of her first pair of knitted mittens. "Oh," I heard myself saying, "she has so much to learn." Yes, they looked like mittens, but they were not so pretty. My first thought was to fix them, but that would rob her of the opportunity to learn. I can better teach her if I offer support (it takes courage to try knitting mittens), provide guidance, point out the errors, and identify alternatives. She's learning. The more she knits, the more mitten details she'll master, and I can be there to help her. Then, when I'm not there, she'll be able to make beautiful mittens on her own.

And finally, I would be hoping that if you were to report on what you'd discovered or had reconfirmed by spending some time with this collection, you would say that there's lots of different activities, assignments, and actions a teacher can take to promote the development of students as learners. We've just pulled up the first bucket from a deep well. Drop it back down into the well of your own experience and expect to come up with more.

Additional Resources from Magna Publications

BULK PURCHASES

To purchase multiple print copies of this book, please visit:
www.MagnaGroupBooks.com

MEMBERSHIPS/SUBSCRIPTIONS

Faculty Focus

www.facultyfocus.com

A free e-newsletter on effective teaching strategies for the college classroom.

The Teaching Professor Membership

www.TeachingProfessor.com

The Teaching Professor is an annual membership that reflects the changing needs of today's college faculty and the students they teach. This new fully online version of the newsletter that faculty have enjoyed for more than 30 years includes the best of the print version—great articles and practical, evidence-based insights—but also many new features including video, graphics, and links that make it an even more indispensable resource.

Academic Leader Membership

www.Academic-Leader.com

Academic Leader covers the trends, challenges, and best practices today's academic decision-makers. Members gain access to the latest thinking in academic leadership and learn how peers at other institutions are solving problems, managing change, and setting direction. New articles are published throughout the month.

CONFERENCES

The Teaching Professor Annual Conference

www.TeachingProfessorConference.com

This event provides an opportunity to learn effective pedagogical techniques, hear from leading teaching experts, and interact with colleagues committed to teaching and learning excellence. Join more than 1,000 educators from around the country.

Leadership in Higher Education Conference

www.AcademicLeadershipConference.com

The Leadership in Higher Education Conference provides higher-education leaders with an opportunity to expand leadership skills with proactive strategies, engaging networking, time-saving tips, and best practices. Attendees hear from a roster of prestigious experts and nationally recognized thought leaders. A broad mix of plenary addresses, concurrent sessions, and timely roundtable discussions leave no topic untouched.

BOOKS

The Academic Leader's Handbook: A Resource Collection for College Administrators

https://www.amazon.com/dp/B0764KMC5Z

The Academic Leader's Handbook: A Resource Collection for College Administrators details an array of proven management strategies and will help further your achievements as a leader in higher education. Discover new leadership tools and insights at departmental, administrative, and executive levels.

Active Learning: A Practical Guide for College Faculty

https://www.amazon.com/dp/B071ZN8R32

Learn how to apply active learning methods in both small and large classes as well as in an online teaching environment. Whether you are new to active learning methods or experienced with them, this comprehensive reference book can guide you every step of the way.

The College Teacher's Handbook: A Resource Collection for New Faculty

https://www.amazon.com/dp/0912150688

The College Teacher's Handbook: A Resource Collection for New Faculty provides the essential tools and information that any new teacher in higher education needs to confidently lead a college classroom.

Essential Teaching Principles: A Resource Collection for Adjunct Faculty

https://www.amazon.com/dp/0912150246

This book provides a wealth of both research-driven and classroom-tested best practices to help adjuncts develop the knowledge and skills required to run a successful classroom. Compact and reader-friendly, this book is conveniently organized to serve as a ready reference whenever a new teaching challenge arises—whether it's refreshing older course design, overcoming a student's objection to a grade, or fine-tuning assessments.

Essential Teaching Principles: A Resource Collection for Teachers

https://www.amazon.com/dp/0912150580

This book serves as a quick and ready reference as you encounter the challenges of teaching college-level material in the high school classroom. For an AP or IB teacher, there's no better resource.

Faculty Development: A Resource Collection for Academic Leaders

https://www.amazon.com/dp/0912150661

Discover proven tips and insights, from top academic experts, that will help you enhance faculty development programming and training on your campus.

Flipping the College Classroom: Practical Advice from Faculty

https://www.amazon.com/dp/B01N2GZ61O

This collection is a comprehensive guide to flipping no matter how much—or how little—experience you have with it. If you are just getting started, you will learn where and how to begin. If you have been at it for a while, you will find new ideas to try and solutions to common challenges. *Flipping the College Classroom: Practical Advice from Faculty* is an invaluable resource that covers all the necessary territory.

Grading Strategies for the Online College Classroom: A Collection of Articles for Faculty

https://www.amazon.com/dp/0912150564

Do your grading practices accurately reflect your online students' performance? Do your assessment and feedback methods inspire learning? Are you managing the time you spend on these things—or is the workload overwhelming? *Grading Strategies for the Online College Classroom: A Collection of Articles for Faculty* can help you master the techniques of effective online grading—while avoiding some of the more costly pitfalls.

Managing Adjunct Faculty: A Resource Collection for Administrators

https://www.amazon.com/dp/B01N2OVK5W

Chances are your adjunct population has been built on an ad hoc basis to fill instructional needs. As a result, your institution might not have a solid management framework to support them. That's a gap you can close with guidance from *Managing Adjunct Faculty: A Resource Collection for Administrators*. This invaluable guide offers an extensive review of best practices for managing an adjunct cohort and integrating them more fully into your campus community.

Teaching Strategies for the Online College Classroom: A Collection of Faculty Articles

https://www.amazon.com/dp/0912150483

Includes online teaching strategies ranging from building a successful start of the semester, fostering productive connections, managing challenging behavior in the online classroom, and enhancing student engagement.

CPSIA information can be obtained
at www.ICGtesting.com
Printed in the USA
LVHW060904200420
653971LV00007B/114